Cut
the unseen cinema

This picture is a mock-up in Life magazine in 1946 (copyright in the photograph, A. L. Schafer) of the Hollywood Code of the time, listing the Ten Commandments of *Thou Shalt Not Show This* in the cinema.

Cut
the unseen cinema
by Baxter Philips

BOUNTY BOOKS
New York

contents

the first sabotage page 7

politics and titillation page 24

in retreat page 50

cut on violence page 88

acknowledgements

Gratitude can only be given for the making of this book to those who have directly or indirectly caused the censorship of films or sequences from them. So this book is affectionately dedicated:
- To the public, which often will not pay to see a good film.
- To the film financiers, who often will not pay to make a good film.
- To the directors, who often fight for the film they want, and to hell with the audience.
- To the stars, who wish to protect their performance at the cost of all other performers – and the film.
- To the distributors, who won't show what they won't show, without giving any reason.
- To the official censors, who have seen and scissored more bad movies (and a few good ones) than the human eye can bear.
- To all, in fact, who have CUT! what we have not been allowed to view.
- To them, THE UNSEEN CINEMA!

the first sabotage

The creation of the world was the first sabotage. Why so, Cioran once asked? Because its creation destroyed the possibility of all other worlds which could be made on this particular planet.

The creation of a film is also a sabotage. It prevents another film being made on the same subject; it uses up on its budget the money which could have made other films; it is completed in a form which is often unsatisfactory to financier, director, distributor and audience. The final print of a film is its first censorship, because it eliminates all other possible versions of that film at that time. As the old Hollywood saying goes, the only positive thing about a film is a negative. In the laboratories lies the unkindest cut of all, the last chance.

Thus censorship in the cinema began with the creation of the cinema in the 1890s. For all that was created by Edison and the Lumière Brothers was a machine which could move the pictures of the habits and inhibitions of their time. Popular entertainment in those days consisted chiefly of the music hall, while Victorian still photography recorded chiefly views of the streets and various female beauties. The music hall already had its censors in France and in England, where the Lord Chamberlain was officially the judge of indecency in the theatre. In Paris, however, the censors were something of a joke. The climax of the can-can, for instance, was the high kick followed by the shrieking splits; as the girls wore nothing under their long petticoats, there was always a flash of thigh and hidden hair. The arts themselves mocked the censorship. Toulouse-Lautrec's friend Ibels drew a whole number of *L'Assiette au Beurre* on the Café Concerts of Paris. It was subtitled 'Censorship' and it proved how far the singers could get away with their risky material. The English Machinson Sisters were perhaps the most suggestive, dancing with skirts hiked high above black stockings and bare thighs, with a live pussy-cat held in the fold of the skirt and with a chorus which went:

Would you give me the tip of it, tip of it,
 tip of it
Would you give me the tip of it, tip of it,
 tip of it
Because I've got a pussy cat
Because I've got a pussy cat
Who hasn't eaten that, that, that!

Ibels took great delight in stamping the words of the song with *Passed By The Censor*.

Toulouse-Lautrec did, in fact, do the cover of *The Motograph Moving Picture Book* of 1895, which featured among other illustrations the Serpentine Dance of Loie Fuller. This dance of the whirling veils above an apparently naked body took its inspiration from Salome, but the transparency of the veils was much helped by backlighting from the new electrical lamps in the theatres. It was another performance of the Serpentine Dance by Loie Fuller's sister under the name of Fatima, which was the hit of Chicago's Columbian Exposition in 1893; this actually led to the first overt act of censorship in the United States, when a peep-show version of it was

Les Sisters Machinson's.

Voulez-vous me donner un bout, bout, bout
Voulez-vous me donner un bout, bout, bout,
Car j'ai un petit chat,
Car j'ai un petit chat,
Qui n'a pas mangé ça, ça, ça!

VISÉ
PAR
LA CENSURE

Gen

anglais

Loie Fuller's dance is taken from *The Motograph Moving Picture Book* of 1895.

Méliès chorus-girls line up behind the moon- rocket.

censored in 1907 by superimposing parallel lines across the print so that the patrons could only see a navel undulating between bars, a sort of Sing-Sing midriff strip show.

In fact, despite the realism of the first film shows of Edison and the Lumière Brothers – trains arriving and workers leaving factories – the early cinema evolved out of the magic tricks of Méliès, who certainly knew the value of a line of chorus girls even on a Trip to the Moon, and out of the popular post-cards and peepshows of the time. For the first cinemas were little more than penny arcades filled with *What The Butler Saw* machines. The films were a series of celluloid images or postcards which flicked over rapidly and gave the illusion of action – usually of a woman undressing under titles such as *In Her Boudoir, The Bridal Chamber, Beware My Husband Comes!* and even *How Bridget Served The Salad Undressed.* They were derived from the popular French postcards of the time and

were animated versions of contemporary titillation – rather like the early years of *Playboy* magazine, they showed everything except pubic hair, in various artistic or fantastic poses. The American postcards of the period tended to be more concerned with clothes and finance; but doubtless each country knew its own market.

If contemporary popular taste determined the nature of the peep-show films for the masses, the making of those films was at first in the hands of their inventors. The Lumière Brothers shot realistic movies and home movies, starring their workers and their families. The public censored them by not attending the later shows and put them out of the film business. George Méliès, essentially a boulevard magician and showman, lasted twenty years in the art of filmed magic shows; but he also was liquidated by lack of public appreciation for his tricks. For he did too few films of ladies in baths and too many of fantastic journeys. He did

The Love Business in the French Postcard

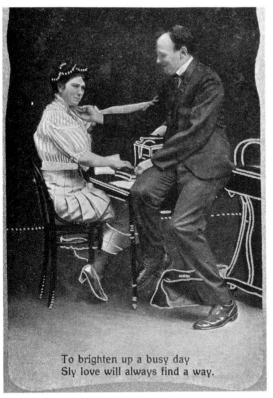

To brighten up a busy day
Sly love will always find a way.

... and the American, with a more commercial approach.

Méliès *Après le Bal – le Tub* (1897) appears to be the first naughty film. He did not follow it up, preferring fantasy voyages like *Le Voyage à travers l'Impossible* (1906).

not discover what the American entrepreneurs discovered – two themes which were to excite both censors and the cinematic public for the next seventy years, a close view of sex and violence.

The two important films in this respect were *The Irwin-Rice Kiss* of 1896 and *The Great Train Robbery* of 1903. In a stage performance of *The Widow Jones,* May Irwin and John C. Rice held a kiss on a stage for a prolonged climax. This kiss was filmed in close-up and led to a huge success, prompting a contemporary critic to complain that the kiss was beastly on stage, but 'magnified to Gargantuan proportions and repeated three times over, it was absolutely disgusting' and called for police interference.

The Great Train Robbery led, indeed, to the invention of modern cinema, with Irwin S. Porter's device of cross-cutting action sequences. But its theme, the actual staging of a robbery with violence, encouraged the making of hundreds of criminal short pictures. Just as the first voyeur films had been based on the popular postcard, so these crime films were based on the penny dreadful series, such as the Buffalo Bill Library or the Jack Sheppard stories, and also on the lurid illustrations in such magazines of contemporary crimes as the *Police Gazette*. But the success of *The Great Train Robbery* led to a spate of recreations of crimes and even executions on the short early movies. Violence had found its market.

Of course, the mob had always been interested in executions. Ballads about the dying words of famous criminals – often in verse – were hawked around the streets of London and Paris before the victim was yet swinging on the rope or headless after the guillotine. Fairground machines showed on animated models the hanging of such famous murderers as Crippen. And on the kinetescope machines in the penny arcades, the audiences could see the actual newsreels of the beheading of a Chinese criminal outside Mukden, the guillotining of four French criminals at Bethune, and the hanging of a man in Missouri. In England, cameras were still forbidden from watching the drop; but a restaging

The hanging of Charles Peace was simulated in fairground style in 1905.

of *The Life of Charles Peace* in 1905 ended with his simulated hanging, performed realistically. Bull-fights and hare-coursing, accident victims, and operations on women were shown in all their gory details, as well as attacks on horses and on children – considered revolting in that order in England. As one disgusted viewer complained in 1909 of a film called *The Black Hand*, two ruffians were actually seen to enter a room where a mother was sewing, 'to take this young child out of its bed, tie a rope round its neck, pass the rope over a peg behind a door, and actually pull the young inno-cent up by the neck until its feet are two or three feet from the floor whilst the mother is kept at bay.'

Official censorship was now at hand because of the second group of censors – after the actual inventors of the process of film-making – the distributors. In France, the grip of the Lumières and Méliès rapidly loosened into the hands of the operators of Gaumont and Pathé, who discovered that the erotic pleased their patrons more than the violent. Borrowing from the lush nudes of contemporary painters such as Bougeaureau and Garnier and Chantron, and also

The Grasshopper by Chantron . . . and a
tableaux vivant of Cupid's Arrow for the naughty
trade.

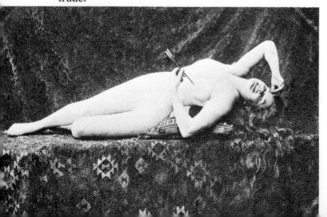

using the tradition of the *tableaux vivants* of undressed ladies in fantastic poses, they ran off a series of naughty film strips under such titles as *The Birth of Venus* (after Botticelli), *The Age for Love,* and *The Model en Déshabille.* Police action after 1905, and growing respectability, put Gaumont and Pathé more into the feature and newsreel business, driving naughty French pictures underground. The Italian cinema, however, began a popular genre which has persisted from the Roman circus through the Middle Ages to the present day – the historical extravaganza featuring naked women under such titles as *Lucrezia Borgia* and *The Last Days of Pompeii,* not to mention Dante's *Divine Comedy,* including naturally all the tortures of hell.

Yet the most important group of film distributors lay in America, and they were a strange medley. After the appearance of the first nickelodeon in 1905, inventors, mechanics, garment manufacturers, shoestring showmen, actors and snake-oil salesmen rushed into the business. Within two years, there were 5,000 official nickelodeons and as many bootleg ones, dealing in Edwardian pornographic movies of the sort recently shown in that interesting compilation by Stern and Neal, *Ain't Misbehavin',* by which a critic was bemused because of 'the many fur-belowed matrons so briskly rogered, and so long ago, for the benefit of the hand-cranked camera.' On Broadway and off it, as Raymon Moley described it, the film business before 1914 resisted academic ordering. Its best description was from the lips of one of its leading figures: 'This isn't a business. It's a dissipation.'

This dissipation became organised for two reasons, first money, then public protest. The amount of films pirated particularly from the Edison Studios forced the leading film-makers and distributors to lease prints of their films rather than to sell them outright and allow unlicensed copies to be struck off the prints. Thus they supported the public outcry against excessively erotic or violent films, which

Medieval woodcuts inspired visions of Dante's Inferno (this still is not from the early Italian film, but the Hollywood remake of 1924).

caused the setting up of a censorship committee in Chicago in 1907 and the temporary closing of all cinema houses in New York shortly afterwards. The outcome of this pressure was the creation of a self-regulating censorship committee among the producers and distributors of films, in order to control their content and their sale. Thus the cash grip on movies was firmly established in the first years of this century, first by the Motion Picture Patents Company, then by the so-called National Board of Censorship, then by the passing of State Laws backed by the local exhibitors for the regulation of films exhibited in each American state.

An orgy from the early Italian *Beatrice Cenci* (1926).

The Vampire's Dance **and the prolonged kiss in** *The Opium Dream* **were the most wicked films on mass release of their time.**

Lya de Putti in a vampish pose.

A similar process took place in all other leading film-making countries, led by France and England, which activated existing censorship provisions and public safety laws to control the infant industry. In England, the First Cinematograph Act of 1909, which dealt mainly with the fire hazards of the new cinemas full of combustible silver-nitrate film stock, was followed by the film manufacturers and renters begging the Home Secretary to set up the British Board of Film Censors, which was duly done. Self-regulation was the plea, in order to increase the profits of the respectable film-makers and to control public protest. Although local borough and county councils could still ban films passed by the Board, on the whole its recommendations and grading of films were accepted country-wide.

In France, the gathering power of the authorities in the realm of censorship led to some absurdities. For instance, the Danish film of 1911, *Vampire's Dance*, was considered too lascivious for Parisian tastes, and the prolonged kissing in Scandinavian films such as *Opium Dream* of 1914, both led to the banning of the film in Paris in 1914 and to the origins of the French myth that somehow sex in the Far North was more scabrous than their own variety. And indeed, not only did Scandinavia create the Vamp in a film of 1911 (so much exploited by its most famous exponents Theda Bara and Lya de Putti) but it also created the first major film on demons, Christiansen's *Witchcraft Through the Ages,* which has never been surpassed in the haunting power of its images by any of the Dracula cycle. In fact, it was so powerful that it was banned from public showing in nearly all countries of the world.

With the onset of the First World War

The Devil comes for his Bride in Christiansen's classic on witchcraft.

and the carnage on the Western Front, there was a definitive rise in censorship in Europe and a general lowering of sexual standards to which film producers catered. It is interesting to note that in the reports of the British Board of Film Censors between 1913 and 1915, new categories arose which caused the Board to request cuts in certain scenes before they could be exhibited with the Board's certificate. For the first time, scenes were now scissored which showed:

The exhibition of profuse bleeding.
Nude figures.
Excessively passionate love scenes.
Bathing scenes passing the limits of propriety.
The drug habit, e.g. opium, morphine, cocaine, etc.
Men and women in bed together . . .

A permissiveness had led to these new scenes being depicted, especially across the Atlantic where those twin methods of showing the naked female body, the Bath

An Edwardian French woman takes a bath in front of her maid . . . followed by Mignon Craig in 1918 and Gloria Swanson in 1919.

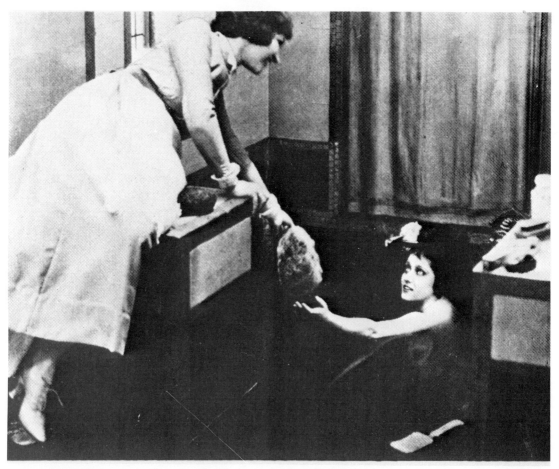

and Love Through the Ages, were becoming increasingly popular. The French had pioneered bathing sequences in drawings, photographs and films. The Americans were quick to follow, careful that the slipping robe and the dark waterline always showed enough and not too much. Physical education and the cult of the New Liberated Woman were given a plunge into reality by the diving films of Annette Kellerman, who eventually shed her one-piece swimsuit entirely in 1916 in *Daughter of the Gods*.

The other method of showing sin acceptable to reformers was by making it biblical and educational and therefore moral. In a story that may be apocryphal,

Annette Kellerman was ready to show far more than the later diving champion Esther Williams, who played the Kellerman life story in Mervyn LeRoy's and Busby Berkeley's *Million Dollar Mermaid* (1952).

Miss Kellerman also seemed to get more out of a waterfall in 1916 than anyone until Busby Berkeley swamped a cascade of beauties in *Footlight Parade* (1933).

one of the first British film exhibitors, Cecil Hepworth, told of getting a parson in 1899 to approve the showing in a church hall of a newsreel of Loie Fuller's famous Serpentine Dance, by blandly telling him that it was a depiction of 'Salome Dancing Before Herod'. In fact, the longest running play in the United States was a graphic description of a drunkard's progress, called *Ten Nights in a Bar-Room*, with a moral ending tacked on, in which the drunkard's good little daughter died of neglect and the prohibitionists saved the wastrel. Although the playing of the piece left nothing to the imagination, it packed in the churchfolk, who loved to see dirty doings in the name of the redemption of sin. The monk Rasputin always used to ask women who protested against seduction by him, 'How can I confess you without your sinning first?' Film-producers also found it profitable to show degradation before salvation, and the film version of *Ten Nights in a Bar-Room* ended in a spectacular brawl. *(See Colour Section)* Even the Emperor Constantine, in an early epic on his life, was shown in pagan orgiastic rule before he could turn devout and Christian in a contemporary moralistic jaunt through the ages called *Man, Woman and Marriage*.

Thus, before the end of the First World War and the coming of the 'art' film through the work of D. W. Griffith and the German Expressionists and the Russian revolutionary film-makers, the main *genres* of films had already been created on the traditions of the past. By that creation, censors had been set up, as if each inventor chose to set up his own executioner. The chaos of the early cinema was soon ordered by its financiers; anarchy quickly gave up to profit.

Moreover, the very traditions of mass entertainment, from which the early cinema grew, hobbled its origins. Thus early producers catered to a conservative public taste and called in censors to regulate their own product, in case they could not make enough money out of it or their excesses banned them off the new screens.

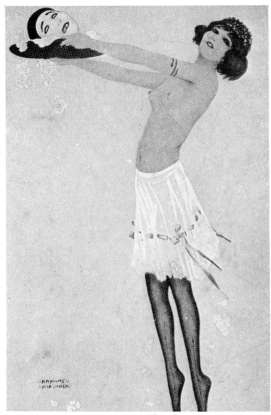

A contemporary French version of Salome
Dancing . . .

The first keyhole shot for peeping toms came
from *Suspense,* an American film of 1913.

The most radical invention of the early
20th century deliberately chained its
limping start. It was to take two decades
of post-war censorship for Ted Cook to
deliver his dictum, 'Motion pictures have
ruined a lot more evenings than they have
morals.' In the intervals, they had to be
made fit for masses and voyeurs.

James Kirkwood plays the Emperor Constantine with his harem in the early *Man, Woman, Marriage.*

politics and titillation

Political censorship began in the First World War. While it was nearly treason to oppose the struggle in France, in the England of 1914 two new categories crept into the Censor's deletions of material – 'Incidents tending to scare the public, and produce panic during the war' and 'Incidents having a tendency to disparage our Allies'. With the rise of socialist theory, 'Relations of Capital and Labour' were considered worthy of the scissors by 1915, and thus political censorship was officially approved as a war measure before the Russian Revolution and the brilliant series of propaganda films made by Eisenstein and others. As the British Board of Film Censors stated clearly in 1921, 'At the risk of appearing to be narrowing the legitimate liberties of the art of the Cinema, the Board has maintained its attitude to what are generally called propaganda films.'

Although Eisenstein's first triumph, *The Battleship Potemkin*, found its way past the censors of the western world through film societies because of its revolutionary montage sequences (then called 'Russian cutting') as much as its revolutionary message, even it suffered the indignity in the United States of losing the picture of Lenin's tomb inscribed with the message – RELIGION IS THE OPIATE OF THE PEOPLE. *Mother*, with its overt call to action, suffered from hacking by foreign distributors as well as outright bars from the censor in many countries. And yet such films as these and *Strike* were deliberate weapons in the agitprop armoury of the Bolsheviks. They did seek to spread Marxism across the world, and when seen, they were a powerful influence. Certainly, Bolshevik Russia banned all unwholesome and capitalist films; if there was something of a reverse ban in effect, the censor was merely being sliced on own scissors. In fact, no Russian film equalled the political bigotry of various 'patriotic' films attacking the Hun or the

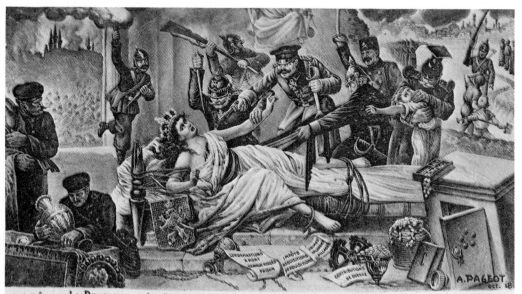

4 AOÛT -1914-   LA BELGIQUE HÉROÏQUE SUBIT LES HORREURS DE L'INVASION ALLEMANDE   28 NOV -1918-
Heroic Belgium suffers the horrors of the german invasion

Three First World War postcards show the high patriotic feeling of France and England, which led to wide powers of censorship of unpatriotic material.

Yellow Peril, such as William Randolph Hearst's infamous serial *Patria* (1917), which Woodrow Wilson himself had sliced up after protests from Japan and Mexico.

As George Bernard Shaw once remarked, the danger of the cinema was not the danger of immorality, but of morality. A desolating romantic morality levelled down most of the products of the cinema, while the over-enthusiastic censorship board of Pennsylvania could claim to rearrange film material into wholesome patterns with the scissors, marrying men off to their mistresses, legitimising bastards, making evil moral. The ridiculous powers of the local state censors in imposing their view of the good of man on the material submitted to them, provoked the first attack on their

The Revolutionary sailors . . . and the repressive Czarist soldiers in the massacre on the Odessa steps from *The Battleship Potemkin* (1925).

powers by America's first major director. In *The Birth of a Nation*, D. W. Griffith has a rabid mulatto called Lynch, attempt to rape Lilian Gish, who is saved by the white knights of the Ku Klux Klan, only to have to throw herself to her death when pursued by another black soldier on the run. Griffith defended his film from the censor's attack by writing a pamphlet called 'The Rise and Fall of Free Speech in America', claiming that film directors had the right to deal with objects that would shock and divide. His next major epic, after some patriotic war movies, where Miss Gish now cringed before the leering Hun, was *Intolerance*, in which Griffith was instructed by the distributors to put more sex into the picture and did so, scouring the red-light districts for some women who would provide nude close-ups for Belshazzar's Feast. These nude shots were later censored and the semi-clothed version shot by his assistant remained, but where Griffith led, de Mille was sure to follow. The Bible would excuse the naked breast.

The American heroes menaced by the Yellow and Revolutionary Peril in *Patria* (1917).

Lilian Gish screams at the threat of rape in *The Birth of a Nation* (1914).

Griffith himself shot Belshazzar's Feast at the moment when Cyrus' final attack on Babylon was about to be mounted (top). His assistant shot extra sequences for the orgy scene (below) as did Griffith himself.

Gloria Swanson indulges herself in *Don't Change Your Husbands* (1919)

. . . and waits to be stripped in *A Society Scandal*, while Stroheim bites the hand that corsets him.

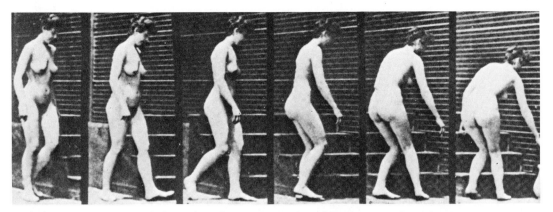

A Muybridge model is a realistic version of the coy undraping of the three nymphs posing for artist Valentino in *The Four Horsemen of the Apocalypse* (1921).

De Mille rose to fame by a series of titillating movies that promised more than they performed, with titles such as *Don't Change Your Husband* and *Male and Female*. In them such new stars as Gloria Swanson acted out the fantasies of the Jazz Babies, even with fauns. Miss Swanson occasionally showed a little much for the scissors, but on the whole, suggestion was all and the title of the film incited without depicting. Contemporary titles in the Jazz Age were such as *Luring Lips, Forbidden Fruit, The Fourteenth Lover, Her Purchase Price, The Good-Bad Wife,* and *A Shocking Night*, with teaser promises for the audience such as 'SEE NECKERS, PETTERS, WHITE KISSES, RED KISSES, PLEASURE-MAD DAUGHTERS, SENSATION-CRAVING MOTHERS . . . THE TRUTH, BOLD, NAKED, SENSATIONAL!'

True perversity on the screen was exploited by the early films of Erich von Stroheim, whose *Blind Husbands* and *Foolish Wives* exposed his penchant for sentimental sadism and even transvestitism. It was a long way from this censored scene of Stroheim in a girdle to the jokey sequence in *Cat Ballou*, where Lee Marvin puts on his corset to go out for his terminal fight against the man with the silver nose. Stroheim very much knew that he had to exploit the title of 'the man you love to hate', just as the male sex symbol of his time, Rudolph Valentino, knew that his role was either as the

Valentino dressing for the bullfight in *Blood and Sand* (1922).

ravisher of the maiden or the spoil of ageing ladies. Although the time-honoured device of the naked artist's model (first used at the invention of the cinematic image in motion by Muybridge) sometimes got a little breast onto a Valentino vehicle, the real power of his films lay in him dressing or menacing or even posing as the naked Pan.

Yet it was not what the stars did on screen but what they did off duty that caused a moralistic solution in young Hollywood. The divorce of Mary Pickford to marry Douglas Fairbanks was bad enough, as was the death of her brother's wife, the Ziegfield Follies' star Olive Thomas, from poison and drug addiction. Other stars confessed to drug habits, but it was popular Fatty Arbuckle who put the scissors to work in Hollywood by his all-night party which ended in the death of Virginia Rappé, a bit-part player. While Arbuckle, after three trials, was exonerated from raping her to death, his career was ruined and Hollywood was alarmed at its own image. A distinguished criminal lawyer who turned down the Arbuckle case warned Hollywood to prepare for tornadoes. Instead, the film barons called in the Postmaster General, Will Hays, to set up a Code, to which Hollywood would ascribe in general in the making of pictures.

Thus public censoriousness of the scandals of the stars led to studio censor-

Keaton gets the better of Arbuckle in *Sherlock Junior* (1924). He always believed in the innocence of his fellow comic.

The Wild Party (1975) takes as its subject another version of the Arbuckle scandal with Virginia Rappé.

Gloria Swanson and Raoul Walsh in *Sadie Thompson* (1928). Later Jean Harlow played the colonial whore role with Clark Gable in *Red Dust* (1932), where she had the obligatory revealing and unrevealing bath in a rain-barrel. A "blue" version of the film with spliced-in sex shots circulated in Havana and in other tourist traps.

ship of the subjects made. The object was to forestall public criticism, and in future, the studios insisted that the stars created by the studios led their private lives publicly according to the images created by the publicity men. Will Hays himself represented the average American, and therefore the mass market, to its middle common denominator. He was, as a contemporary commentator said, 'as indigenous as sassafras root. He is one of us. He is folks . . . He is a human flivver, the most characteristic native product.' So Mr. Hays set out to make the films of Hollywood into America's second most characteristic native product.

Hays did this by cajoling, persuading and browbeating nearly all of Hollywood into accepting a rough Code of Standards, called the Formula of 1924, which pledged the Motion Picture Producers and Distributors to try and avoid the teasing title, the wrong subject, the scandalous film. In that year, the Hays Code got sixty-seven popular books or plays dropped as film projects. But this effort at self-regulation soon faded. By 1926, only ten subjects were dropped, and Hays himself had to let *Rain* (retitled as *Sadie Thompson*) and *They Knew What They Wanted* go out, and such British black-leg imports as *White Cargo*, which invented a new form of pulling in the crowds by advertising itself as the picture 'banned by Will Hays'.

If Hollywood self-regulation of the subject material was only moderately successful, the censors in the individual states had a chopping block of opportunities in regulating the final product. Ernst and Lorenz in their 'Censored: The Private Life of the Movies' worked out that the State censors in 1928 made 1,672 cuts in film sequences dealing with crime, 872 cuts in sexy scenes, 348 cuts for impropriety, but only 49 cuts for attacks on the government and 10 cuts for attacks on religion. Forbidden words were 'bum', 'bitch', 'chippy', 'mistress', 'harlot', 'naked', 'prostitute', – forbidden phrases were 'it wasn't love', 'long, lonely

Clark Gable rigs up a screen between his twin bed and Claudette Colbert's in *It Happened One Night* **(1934), thus avoiding the censor's scissors and winning an Oscar. Gable referred to the intervening blanket as "the Walls of Jericho" – not till marriage did the trumpets blow and the blanket come tumbling down. This twin-bed convention was strangely contrasted to French tradition that happy living meant going to bed together, even in the Puritan days of the First World War.**

Conrad Nagel kisses Garbo in *The Mysterious Lady* (1928).

nights', and even 'twin beds', despite the Hollywood tradition of always putting married couples in twin beds for fear that they might seem to occupy the same one. Kisses could not last for more than four feet of film wherever the shoulder straps or hands were. No actor could thumb his nose, slap a woman's behind, live with a girl, use profanity, or discuss pregnancy, venereal disease, birth control, abortion, eugenics, illegitimacy, prostitution, miscegenation, or divorce. And not until Hedy Lamarr appeared naked in *Ecstasy* did a major actress play in the nude. The bathing sequence of the film was, of course, nominally banned in the United States, although not in Germany or France. Ironically, prints of it became rare due to Miss Lamarr's later marriage to a wealthy man, who tried to impose his own censorship by buying up all extant copies of the film. Time so changed that when the bathing sequence was reshown in the compilation called *The Love Goddesses*, it seemed almost innocent compared with more recent scenes of strip and rape.

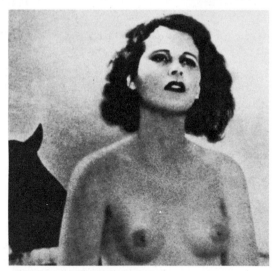

Hedy Lamarr in the woods and the water in *Extase* (1933).

Yet the governing morals of the American Cinema were bound to break any truly erotic or perverse film-maker, and break Stroheim they did. The story of his quarrels with the studios began with his endless shooting of *Greed* − necessarily mutilated by the distributors because it ran for nine hours and would have been impossible for them to distribute. His subsequent overshooting of the orgy sequences in *The Merry Widow*, with Nubian servants in chastity belts and a masked naked female orchestra, was duplicated in *The Wedding March*, which itself culminated by an attempted rape in a slaughterhouse. Paramount cut two successful pictures out of enough footage for four films. Stroheim's last extravaganza, *Queen Kelly* with Gloria Swanson, ended incomplete with Miss Swanson (acting as star and producer) firing Stroheim after

Lamarr floats in *The Love Goddesses*.

The female orchestra from *The Merry Widow* (1925), also censored.

This shot of ZaSu Pitts getting into bed in *Greed* (1923), was marked 'Suppressed' by Stroheim himself.

The beginning of the rape sequence in the slaughterhouse in *The Wedding March* (1927).

The outrageous Queen of the Brothels whipping Gloria Swanson in *Queen Kelly* (1928).

The image of decadent Germany from *The Testament of Dr. Mabuse* (1932).

The beggars get ready to insult the Queen in *The Threepenny Opera* (1931).

she found that she was meant to end as the madam of a chain of brothels, owned by a perverted queen who liked to wear only an angora coat and take long baths and whip Miss Swanson out of her marble halls. Stroheim's producers savaged his films even before the censors shortened them to snippets. In fact, Stroheim's largest sin in Hollywood was his prolixity, not his perversity. He cost too much and was eliminated as a director.

That was also Eisenstein's problem when he came to work in Hollywood. At first he fell foul of the Hays Office in his choice of a subject, Dreiser's *An American Tragedy*. And when he found a group of private backers to support him, led by the radical novelist Sinclair Lewis, he played Stroheim, shooting *Que Viva Mexico!* endlessly south of the border, and offending the morality of his puritan American producers by showing women with naked breasts and pseudo-religious blasphemous scenes including a travesty of a crucifixion. He was not allowed to edit the final version of his film, and three versions have been issued from his material, with other versions possible to follow from other cineastes. The cutting room is the final censorship of the director.

The studio system world-wide did, indeed, triumph over the obsessions of the directors, except where perversity was encouraged, as in Weimar Germany. There the artistic success of *The Cabinet of Dr. Caligari* led to a thorough portrayal of most human perversions and follies and murders in such masterpieces as the Mabuse films (banned by some American state boards for portraying anarchy), *Waxworks, Pandora's Box, The Threepenny Opera* (banned in France as subversive), and such minor pieces as the homosexual *A Man's Girlhood* and the transves-

tite *Prince Von Pappenheim*. Louise Brooks, who played the tease in American comedies, was transformed by Pabst into one of the most erotic creatures ever to haunt the screen, while in a curious reversal, the American von Sternberg was imported to direct and make Marlene Dietrich into the archetype of the man-degrading woman. While both Brooks and Dietrich never stripped, their suggestion of evil was so total that the films were usually cut or banned to the limited screening of film societies.

The only truly erotic revolt of the cinema lay in that outburst of genius known as the Surrealist Cinema. Follow-

Louise Brooks is the Femme Fatale in *Pandora's Box* (1928).

Marlene Dietrich degrades Emil Jennings in *The Blue Angel* (1930).

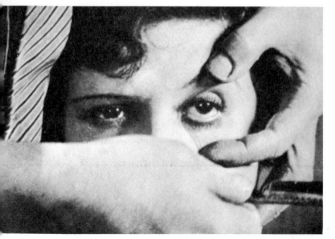

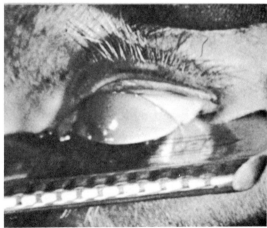

The razor slashes the eyeball in *Un Chien Andalou* (1928).

ing René Clair's pioneering *Entr'acte*, Buñuel's *Un Chien Andalou* and *L'Age d'Or* showed sexual violence and savagery on screen that was censored in most countries until recent times. The razor-slash of an eyeball, the androgyne's walking-stick picking at the severed wrist, the agony of bloody love and the sucking of hands, the succession of raw images produced by Buñuel still disturb and shock after forty years, more than any of those of his imitators including Jadorowski. He first showed the violence of sex, the outrage of sex within a bourgeois society. Surrealist Cinema gave us the nightmare images of our era.

The assault of the Surrealist film-makers was limited by small distribution, low budgets and mass indifference. The cinema audiences preferred the conventions of their time. In France, the brilliant

and inventive Abel Gance, who was capable of the early distortions of *La Folie de Dr. Tube* and of the split screen of *Napoleon*, was reduced to conventional bare-breasted orgy pictures in the Italian mode such as *Lucrezia Borgia*. Fascism in Italy, indeed, had brought a puritan influence to the cinema outside the historical spectacle, where slave-girls were still allowed to flaunt what they had.

The Great Depression, however, brought other results in the United States, where the Hays Code took a beating from the new sex goddesses and choreographers. The rise of Garbo and Harlow in their satin suggestions kept the small town censors to their hackwork, as in the massage sequence in Harlow's *Platinum Blonde* (1931). Yet the increasing excesses of the other crowd-pulling genre, the horror film, began to attract a larger

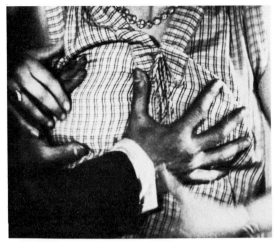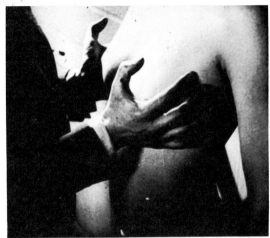

The hands paw at the woman's breasts and she suddenly becomes naked in *Un Chien Andalou.*

The lover sucks at his own hands, his beloved sucks at his hands . . . and at the toe of the marble statue in *L'Age d'Or* (1930).

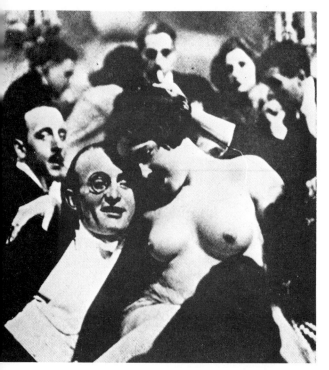

share of censorship. Its genius, Tod Browning, had gone too far, progressing from subjects such as an armless knife-thrower and good-bad Siamese Twins to *Freaks*, the one indisputable masterpiece of the circus cinema. Its true and affecting portrayal of the deformed and midget circus performers was killed worldwide by censorship, while such titillatory extravaganzas as de Mille's *Sign of the Cross* (1932) could get away with Claudette Colbert in her bath of asses' milk and the near-naked Elissa Landi menaced with rape by a gorilla. It was also almost unique in the history of censorship by having additions when reissued in 1942. In that version, the American air-force dropped leaflets on Rome, while carrying two clergymen who just happened to be thinking of the past of the Eternal City. Then, hey presto, cut from the new steel Airmen of the Apocalypse to the old *Sign of the Cross*, which ended with the winged angels of the Flying Fortresses

Orgy scenes from Abel Gance's *The End of the World* (1931) and *Lucrezia Borgia* (1935).

Harlow telephones from the massage parlour in *Platinum Blonde* (1931). Garbo tempts the devil idol in *Mata Hari* (1932).

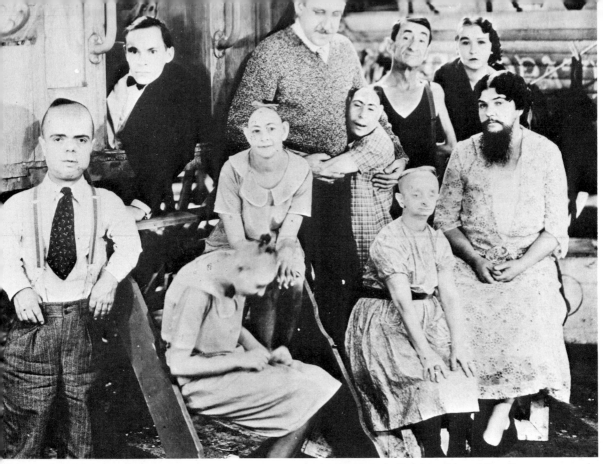

Tod Browning with his friends, the circus performers, who perform in *Freaks* at the wedding-feast between the midget and the circus lady.

Claudette Colbert in her bath and Elissa Landi at the stake in *Sign of the Cross*.

Lina Basquette proves her atheism in *The Godless Girl* (1929), while Marie Prevost goes behind bars for her delinquency.

departing from the smoke of burned Rome.

Perhaps the funniest incident of reverse censorship was the Russian showing of another of de Mille's films, the evangelist tear-jerker, *The Godless Girl* (1929). In that, the Russian censors released the film, which was very popular among the Bolsheviks, with the last reel missing, thus leaving the godless girl unredeemed after all her sinning and showing atheism spreading fast among the American young. Yet back at home, de Mille at least paid lip-service to biblical and Hays Code ethics. It was the open contempt shown for the Code by Harlow and even more Mae West that spurred on a new bout of morality through a boycott of 'Condemned Films' organised by the National Legion of Catholic Decency. This caused such a dip in the box-office takings that the leading American distributors did not show a single Condemned film for the seven years after 1936, and even set up the Breen Office to put a seal of approval on those films which stuck by the Hays Code, thus qualifying for national distribution. The League also attacked fiercely the tease-posters of unlicensed films such as *Marihuana (See Colour Section)* and tried to get them banned by State or city film boards. Other unlicensed films made by such producers as the Sonney Brothers for the semi-blue film market occasionally achieved a measure of class. *Child Bride*, for instance, had sequences that echoed *The Birth of a Nation* and foretold *Baby Doll*, where the young schoolmistress is stripped and flogged by the Klan for defending the nymphet, happily inciting her cousin at the swim-hole.

The new public pressure and self-regulation by Hollywood did lead to the decline of the fabulous Mae West with her double entendres, so lethal in the new age of sound films. She flouted accepted morality; in the famous courtroom scene of *My Little Chickadee*, she was accused of showing contempt of court and replied, 'I'm trying to hide it'. She did not hide anything, and she was condemned for it by Hollywood in one of its periodic fits of cleansing.

Licensed to titillate, however, was the legendary Busby Berkeley, who used the stage tradition of the underdressed chorine to get away with every breach of the Code possible and still get the seal of approval. He used silhouettes to show

nudity in *Gold Diggers of 1933* in a way that was not to be used again till Martine Carol took a famous shower in *Nathalie* in 1957. His Sign of the Cross was a group of chorus girls, showing their legs and headdresses. He could put naked girls in chains in *Roman Scandals* (1933) and spread their legs about a giant cherry in *Dames* (1934). He even got away with the notorious giant banana and strawberry sequence in *The Gang's All Here* (1943), although Brazil banned the picture. In this, lines of chorus girls dressed in the Copacabana style with bare midriffs supported yellow six-foot bananas on their pelvises, making these drooping erections nod up and down like a heavenly gang rape. The climax of the

number was a high aerial shot, in which the bending bananas all formed in a shape suspiciously like a hairy oval, which suddenly opened up to reveal a circle of near-naked chorus girls lying back with their legs apart enfolding several giant strawberries; then came the pecking bananas again and buried them from sight. The number ended with Carmen Miranda belting out her song under a sky full of bunches of bananas, with

glistening red strawberries making a guard of honour for her in a slow track-back down the passageways of desire. If such numbers could pass the censors without a cut, more suggestive and vulgar than any nudity, it showed that somehow the dance redeemed all, because it was as unreal as a stage show or a night out.

On the other hand, *M*, *Maedchen in Uniform*, *La Maternelle*, and *Carnival in Flanders* were hacked about until their plots disappeared into the scissors of American decency.

By the end of the 1930s, the newest and worst form of political censorship was rising in Europe. Stalin's Russia had cut

The patterns Leni Reifenstahl drew out of Nazi formations and the Olympics of 1936 were the patterns of the coming war for the domination of the *Third Reich*.

up Eisenstein's late career, imposed the image of the Dictator into all contemporary Russian films, and literally killed or sent to Siberia any dissidents in the arts. Nazi Germany had also imposed a ruthless censorship on anything held to be decadent, eliminating and burning all of Weimar Germany's extraordinary contribution to an Expressionist Cinema. Leni Riefenstahl was the Busby Berkeley of the Nazi Movement, photographing the patterns and the pomp of the Third Reich's spectacles as extravagantly and formally as the master of dance choreography. The final hilarious parody of the style was in *The Producers*, once titled *Springtime for Hitler*, where the chorusgirls stomp round in a swastika pattern.

The Second World War began as the First World War had ended, with political censorship more important than other varieties of suppression. As Ernst and Lindey wrote in 'The Censor Marches On' in 1940, 'Fear of sex is on the wane.

Busby Berkeley drilled his performers in their version of patriotism too in *Gold Diggers in Paris* (1938), and *Babes in Arms* (1939).

The new spectre is "subversive" ideas'. The hilarious case of the period was the Russian film on the persecution of the Jews by the Nazis, *Professor Mamlock*. Before the Soviet-Nazi non-aggression pact, it was banned in England as 'too political', although shown in the Soviet Pavilion at the New York World's Fair. After the pact, it was authorised in London and banned at the Soviet Pavilion. The pro-Loyalist *Spain in Flames* was banned by many American States as defending a government that killed priests; in New Jersey, although it was against Franco, it was banned under the Anti-Nazi Law. Yet, as Ernst and Lindey pointed out, political censorship was minor compared with public indifference. Good films such as *Abraham Lincoln*, *The Informer*, *Emperor Jones*, *Greed* and *Hallelujah* had lost money at the box-office and did not encourage producers to make their like. At the last resort, the cash receipts of the capitalist film were more powerful than creator, distributor or censor. If the public did not always get what it wanted, it got rid of what it did not want. The crowd was the last sabotage.

Walter Huston fights for the right as the young reformer and awaits his assassination as the President in D. W. Griffith's *Abraham Lincoln* (1930).

in retreat

As the Second World War largely destroyed the ethical code and assumptions of Europe and to a lesser degree of the United States, so the slow erosion of the Hollywood Code began. There was a battle about the adultery and murder in *The Postman Always Rings Twice*, but the film was made. And when Howard Hughes put out an outrageous publicity campaign for Jane Russell in *The Outlaw* and the Breen Office revoked its seal of approval, Hughes still distributed the picture in 1946 and packed in the audiences, especially when a judge declared that the breasts of Jane 'hung over the picture like a thunderstorm spread over a landscape.' War had broken down the old barriers and money called in the new change. After the shots of naked girls raped and carved to pieces by the German army in Anatole Litvak's *The Battle of Russia*, and the realism of the torture sequences in the new Italian wave of war films such as *Paisan* and *Rome, Open City*, the documentary of life seemed stronger than the ethics of escapism.

There was also the matter of millions of American troops experiencing European and Asian manners and women. The realism of the love scenes played by Gerard Philipe in *Le Diable au Corps* might still be scissored in the Anglo-Saxon

Jane Russell lounges with a suggestive revolver in this poster from *The Outlaw* (1946). It is interesting to see the similar layout of the Bond poster in *Thunderball* (1965). In twenty years, male nudity had become possible.

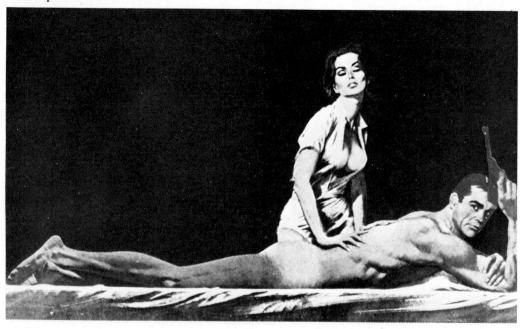

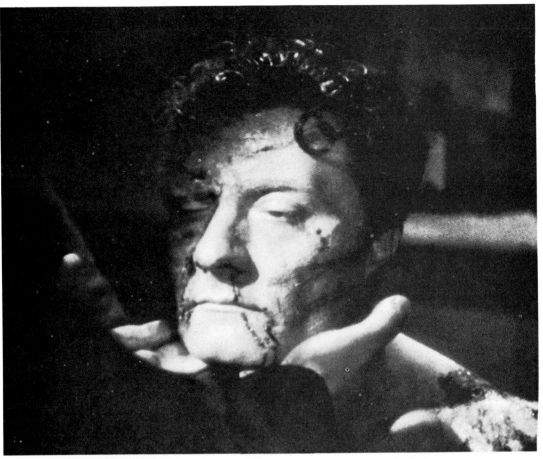

The torture of Manfredi, from *Rome, Open City* (1945). Its sickening realism was to influence two other films of soldiers and partisans and torture sequences . . .

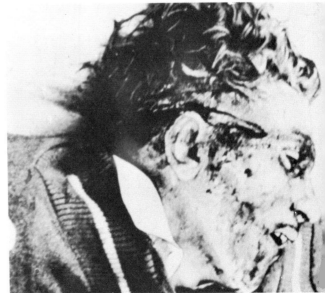

Godard's *Le Petit Soldat* (1961) and Pontecorvo's film, *Battle of Algiers* (1966) – both of which were banned in France.

The beach kiss in *From Here to Eternity* (1953). There were two scenes scissored from the picture by studio chief Harry Cohn, but only of Montgomery Clift thinking the attackers at Pearl Harbour were Germans and composing a blues on his bugle.

countries; but they would influence the famous beach love scene that was a landmark of the American cinema in 1953, Deborah Kerr's grapple with the surf and Burt Lancaster in *From Here to Eternity*, appropriately a war picture. Some British movies like *Brighton Rock* might be hacked by the American censor because of the cold seduction by Pinkie of the girl witness of the crime; but in general the largest outcry of the immediate postwar years was against the 'unpatriotic' Charles Chaplin. A paternity suit and a Mann Act charge brought against him caused ripples of an Arbuckle-type witch-hunt, while he chose to shake

Hollywood's gold dust off his feet after making the bitter and mocking *Monsieur Verdoux* with its implication that private murders were nothing beside war massacres, using the terrible line, 'Millions sanctify!' The refusal of the American and British distributors to show this film widely caused its effective suppression outside France.

The Italian cinema was as outspoken about sex as about torture, and the near-rape of Silvana Magnano by Vittorio Gassman in *Bitter Rice* in 1949 was paral-

Sophia Loren first appeared in a silly extravaganza called *Era Lui, Si, Si.*

Loren also played in such undistinguished epics as *Madame* and Hollywood failures such as *Boy on a Dolphin* before reaching stardom and keeping herself covered for the censor.

54

Martine Carol did not bother about the asses' milk in *Sins of the Borgias*.

leled in shock by the elopement of the
married Ingrid Bergman with Roberto
Rossellini, who directed her, pregnant by
him, in *Stromboli*. Heavily cut by its
appalled American backers and distributors, it proved more of a damp squib
than a volcano. Bergman herself was cold-
shouldered for many years for her be-
haviour – and for the flop of the film –
and it took her a decade of playing good
women again to re-establish herself in the
annals of morality and the mass distribution circuits.

More traditional for Italian movies
were the bare-breasted sequences in
historical epics, in which some of the later
stars of the world cinema were to appear,
such as Sophia Loren. The fashion was
followed in France, where Martine Carol
played Lucrezia Borgia and became the
most famous bather in history after
Claudette Colbert; even Jeanne Moreau
played a lecherous queen in *La Reine
Margot*, before her sensational on-screen
apparent orgasm in *Les Amants* launched
her to international stardom. Where
naked historical scenes were necessary for

**Jeanne Moreau also began as a mere historical
figure.**

the plot, the trick of the double version of a take was developed after the
Roman circus sequence in *Fabiola* in 1948;
in this, the hordes of naked girls acting
as fodder for the lions or dangling from
crosses became mysteriously clothed or
invisible in the American and British
versions of the film. When the rise of
television, indeed, imposed its own censorship on old movie material and decided
what was suitable for home viewing, it
also became commercially important to
shoot a less torrid version of sequences

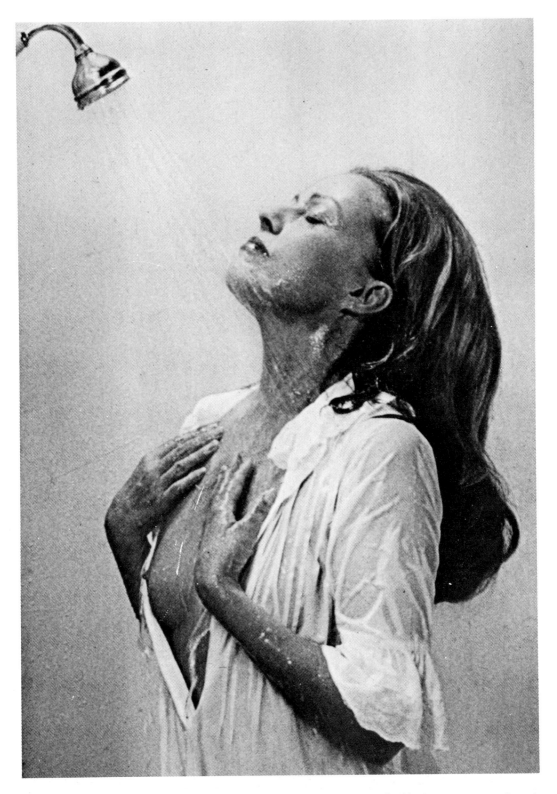

. . . but she remained a creature of her time who denied time, as can be seen in this shower sequence from the recent de Broca film, *Chère Louise*.

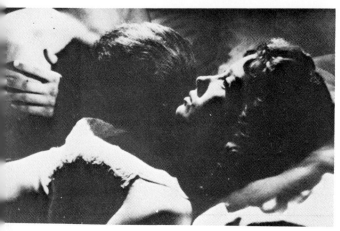

The American and the European version of the bed sequence from *Cry Tough*.

for the areas of heavy censorship, such as American television, Spain and South Africa.

Hollywood itself accepted the idea of a double version and double vision 'to get a little more mileage out of it in Europe.' In a famous sequence in *Cry Tough*, a film about juvenile delinquency set in the early fifties, the American producers got Linda Cristal to strip off for the bed scene for Europe, and to play it clothed for home consumption. What was especially ludicrous about the American version of the scene was that John Saxon had to keep his knees on the floor throughout the bed sequence to keep in line with the Hollywood Code of the time, in case love actually put him on the same sheets as Miss Cristal.

Such hypocrisy could not last, especially as the dull and successful competition of television forced the Hollywood movie to become more daring; meanwhile the Supreme Court decision of 1952 in the case of Rossellini's *The Miracle* weakened censorship by the Legion of Decency and gave to films the protection of the free speech clause in the First and Fourteenth Amendments to the Constitution. The way back to the box-office was to shock. All accounts of the fifties show that Brando's rape sequence from *A Streetcar Named Desire,* and the playing of *Baby Doll* by Carroll Baker were probably more destructive to the Breen Office than anything else. Tennessee Williams alone – the author of both original stage plays – seemed to have upended the unrealism of sex in Hollywood, although his Southern world of melodrama and homosexuality and violence was itself unreal. When a Broadway poster, forty-five yards long, showed Carroll Baker sucking her thumb in her crib a few blocks down from the Legion of Decency, Catholic outrage knew no bounds – but still failed to get the Breen Office to rescind its Seal of Approval. In fact, the Legion now began to retreat and to

As late as the 1960s, Elke Sommer was shot both naked and clothed for different markets in Forman's *The Victors* (1963).

Brando repels Vivien Leigh, playing Blanche, before raping her in *Streetcar Named Desire* (1951).

invent new categories of acceptability to allow adult Catholics after 1957 to view such films as *La Dolce Vita* and *Lolita*.

The erosion of censorship in the United States and the rise of the independent producer, largely free from studio control and Hays Code censorship of the shooting script, was paralleled elsewhere. In England, nudity was allowed in 1953 in an inoffensive and unerotic little film about an ageing man converted from

Carroll Baker began in her crib with her husband as the voyeur in *Baby Doll* (1956).

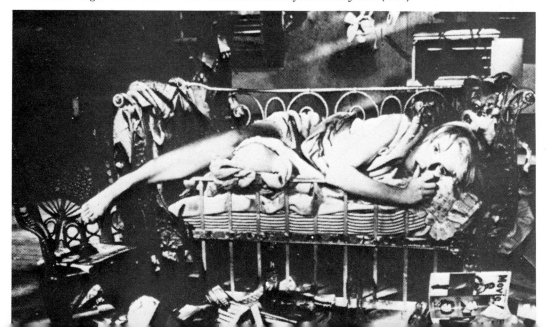

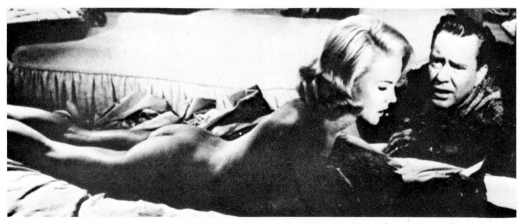

She soon grew up and progressed to indifferent movies such as *Sylvia,* and now plays in such vehicles as *Baba Yaga,* an Italian film about a strip-cartoon witch, from which these stills come.

miserliness to generosity by going to a nudist camp. It was called *The Garden of Eden* and had female nudes in colour, all in the name of a serious devotion to being bare. This new permissiveness led to a flood of nudist films, which inevitably grew boring because of their archness, until the new king of titillation and the soft-core movies arose, Russ Meyer, with his successful *The Immoral Mr. Teas,*

made in four days, soon to be followed by *Not Tonight, Henry,* a merry romp through history where the hero imagined himself an all-conquering Napoleon and an amorous John Smith faced with a choice of Indian maidens. These sex-ploitation films were cut decreasingly through the sixties, until they became commonplace and were yawned off the screen.

The rich wife does a bored strip-tease in *La Dolce Vita* (1959).

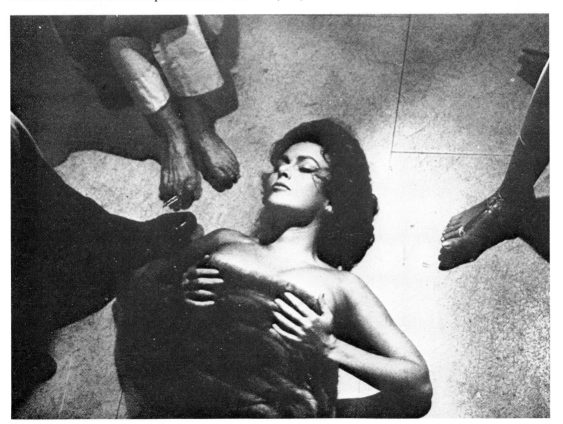

60

The Immoral Mr. Teas and Henry's choice in
Not Tonight, Henry.

In France, however, the New Wave directors led by Godard and Louis Malle pushed back the frontiers of sex and violence on the screen. If Anna Karina and Jeanne Moreau became the darlings of the art houses, Brigitte Bardot became the international symbol of the sex kitten, displacing Carroll Baker and the Sue Lyon of *Lolita* from male fantasies by her explicit sexuality. In one famous scene in *Love is my Profession*, she lifted her shirt to Jean Gabin to tempt him – the scissors saved the Anglo-Saxon world from seeing the scene. Usually, though, audiences saw her in the old tease-roles, as in the shawl dance of *A Woman Like Satan*. Of twenty-seven French films totally condemned by the Legion of Decency, seven starred Brigitte Bardot.

It was Sweden, though, which lived up to its reputation as the shocker of the Far North. In the fifties, two streams of influence trickled down like melting icebergs, slowly washing away the reserves of the moralists of the world. The innocence of young love in Sweden progressed from the charm of *One Summer of Happiness* (1951), which played uncut in Paris and even in some American states, to the outright sexualities and

Bardot tempts Gabin – and plays with a shawl.

frontal nudities of the more permissive age of the late sixties, shown in *I am Curious Yellow*. The other stream lay in the brooding and obsessive work of Ingmar Bergman, so obviously an 'art' director that his double rape scene in *The Virgin Spring* could force the censor to accept it uncut outside Britain and some American states. It was the same for Kurosawa's rape scene in *Rashomon*, which brought the Japanese cinema international notice, although it was again an 'art' film. It represented in a historical and acceptable form a Japanese local cinema of sado-masochistic violence, which was to become the most extreme and censorable in the world, escalating through the rape-scene in *Onibaba* to its present excesses.

The scissors, indeed, became blunted by the atrocities shown by the war news-

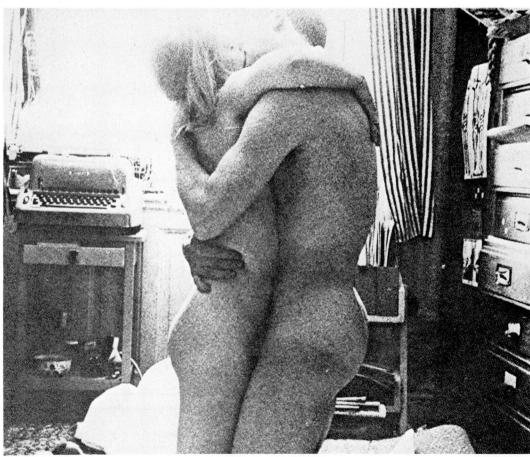

One Summer of Happiness (above) gives way to *I am Curious-Yellow*.

The wife is raped by the bandit in *Rashomon* (1950). The samurai-killer is raped in *Onibaba* (1964) (below)

The circular pods open in *Invasion of the Body Snatchers* (1956).

An early American poster of moralism and violence.

A 1930's teaser American poster.

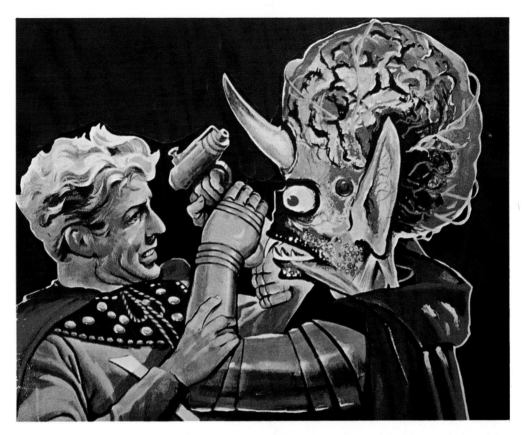

Flash Gordon, the hero of the 1930s (brilliantly drawn by Gogos and reproduced by permission of the Warren Publishing Company) is now camped up in *Flesh Gordon,* the space-traveller to the planet Porno in 1975.

Sex, blasphemy and violence escalate to the ultimate in these modern scissored sequences from *The Devils* and *Death Walks in High-Heeled Shoes*.

The custard pies fly in _Dr. Strangelove_ (1963).

reels in every home that had a television set. The history of censorship after the late fifties is one of a slow retreat for two decades. No ground lost is ever regained. No permission given is ever taken back. Thus the unseen cinema of one year, the sequences cut out by the official censors, were likely to be displayed by a fuller version of the film shown on its re-issue some years later. What was never replaced were the sequences cut out by the egos of the stars, directors or studio bosses, such as the Buster Keaton sequence in _Limelight_ which was truncated because it had competed with the master Charles Chaplin himself, the humour in _Invasion of the Body-Snatchers_, because it was meant to conflict with the horror of the people-pods, and the custard-pie fight in _Dr. Strangelove_, because Kubrick himself thought its farce took away from the sick joke of the dropping of the Bomb. One strange replacement did, however, take place from a studio which never went back on anything – Disney. When the commercial flop, _Fantasia_, suddenly be-

came a cult film for the Flower Power generation (the best 'turn-on' in town), it was re-issued to box-office success in its full length, having once been chopped through financial pressures to two-thirds of Disney's intentions.

If the unofficial censors – the makers and stars and distributors and backers of the films – still exercised their whims and blades of steel, the official hackers fought a slow retreat that makes Mao's Long March look like a sprint to the North of China. Most indicative of their loss of power was the way in which they treated various themes in films throughout the sixties and seventies – in particular, rape, torture, and perversion. At each point, where the 'art' film led the way, the exploitation film was bound to follow and to appeal to an audience which demanded more and more explicit savagery on-screen to get it to leave the television set at home. It was no longer a case of 'How Do You Keep 'Em Down On The Farm Now That They've Seen Paree', but a case of how do you keep 'em coming

Valentino eyes the audience before attending to Agnes Ayres in *The Sheik* (1921).

to the movies now that the box is for free.

Rape was the first answer. Unshown in *The Birth of a Nation*, implied by Valentino in *The Sheik*, excised from the flashbacks in *Carnival in Flanders*, it was half-depicted in *Of Mice and Men* in 1939 – a Steinbeck novel on film could get away with that sort of thing. *Johnny Belinda* in 1948 also was too explicit about the rape of the deaf-and-dumb Jane Wyman, and got the producer sacked from Jack Warner's studio. Claire Bloom's gang-rape was also cut from the *Chapman Report*, although seen in the preview in San Francisco. Its director, Cukor, recalled with nostalgia, 'A fast series of cuts of pushing, shoving, grabbing, falling, gasping, arms, legs . . .', but the studio chief Zanuck cut it all the same – and the film did not work. Nor did Miss Bloom's more explicit rape by Paul Newman in that minor outrage of a remake of *Rashomon* in 1964, *The Outrage*.

Rape is now both explicit and commonplace in film. The gang-rape by Moroccan soldiers of Sophia Loren and her teenage daughter in de Sica's *Two Women*

In Marty Ritt's remake of *Rashomon*, Laurence Harvey is the husband bound to the tree, while Paul Newman assaults his wife, Claire Bloom.

got by most of the censors because of the tradition of Italian neo-realism, and the reputation of author Moravia and of the director himself. In England, too, the growth of the 'kitchen sink' English cinema led to more graphic depictions of sexual enjoyment in *Room at the Top* and sexual violence from Peter Collinson in *Penthouse* and in *Fright*. Of the first film, the British censor wrote that he could only 'hope that this film caused no harm to anyone.' Yet pass it he did.

Certain rapes, however, were too violent for the screen. Popeye's rape of

Sophia Loren tries to comfort her daughter after their rape in *Two Women* (1960).

Suzy Kendall gets raped imaginarily and visually in *Penthouse,* while Ian Bannen is the psychotic murderer and rapist in *Fright* where Susan George is the sufferer (below).

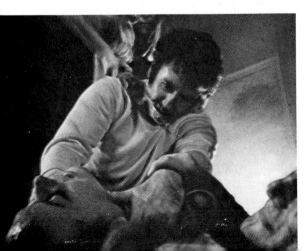

The girls play with the photographer in
Blow-Up (1966).

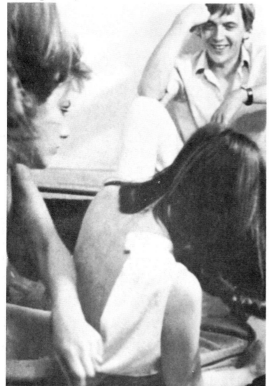

Malcolm McDowell at last gets his girl in *If . . .*
(1968).

Oliver Reed and Allan Bates have a naked
wrestle in *Women in Love* (1969).

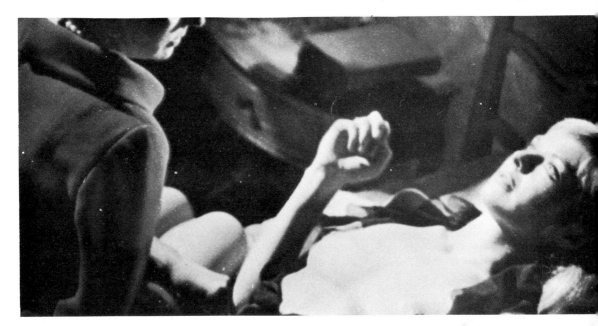

Temple Drake with a corncob pipe in both versions of William Faulkner's *Sanctuary*, that of 1933 and of 1960, were both glossed over, although essential to the meaning of the film – and both versions failed as a result. On the other hand, the more that sexual play and near-rape became acceptable through the 'art' film, the more it became the common jargon of the second-rate cinema. *Blow-Up* was a trend-setting film in this respect in 1966. In a photographer's studio sequence, David Hemmings romped with the naked Jane Birkin and Gillian Hills, and the pubic hair of the nymphets was allowed to appear on screen in England because of 'the film's quality and integrity.'

Where art goes, exploitation is sure to follow, not to mention more art. The naked wrestling scene became almost obligatory for the 'good' British movie, from the lovers in *If* to the two men struggling in Ken Russell's *Women In Love*. Widely censored in Spain and other unpermissive countries, the success of these scenes led to more explicitness in the cinema than ever, from the lesbianism in *The Killing of Sister George* to the overt homosexuality of *Boys in the Band*, and the male rape and drag of *Fortune and Men's Eyes*. Probably the most explicit of the

Susannah York plays a lesbian love scene with Beryl Reid in *The Killing of Sister George* (1969).

The prisoner in drag incites the other prisoners in *Fortune and Men's Eyes* (1971) in a strip routine.

rape scenes to get by in a serious film on general release in America was the assault on the dumpy virgin Cathy by her teenage friends in Frank Perry's *Last Summer*.

At a lower level, the schoolboy rebellions of Vigo's anarchic *Zero de Conduite* degenerated to the attempted rape of the teacher's wife by a gang of schoolboys in *Unman, Wittering and Zigo*, and the actual rape of the schoolteacher in di Leo's *Sex in the Classroom* and in the Swedish mock-documentary Engell's *Schoolday*. The same was true in the Western. The off-screen rape of Marlene

The bored girl-friend incite the two boys to rape Cathy in *Last Summer* (1969).

Dietrich in Lang's *Rancho Notorious* of 1952 became the on-screen rape of Isela Varga by Kris Kristofferson in Peckinpah's *Bring Me The Head of Alfredo Garcia* of 1974. The teaser poster came back in its full glory, as in a film simply called *The Rape*, which was issued an X certificate by the Greater London Council's censorship committee, without being passed by the British Board of Film Cen-

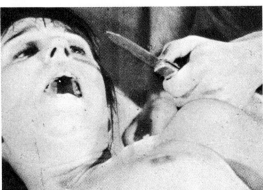

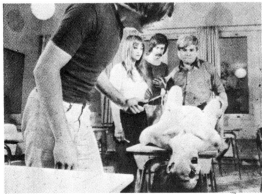

The teacher is assaulted in *Sex in the Classroom* (1974) and in *Schooldays* (1975), both unshown in England. Kristofferson rapes the prostitute in Peckinpah's 1974 western (below).

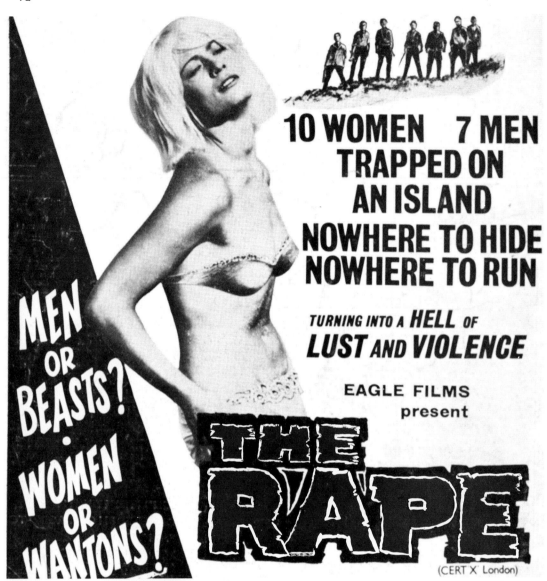

10 WOMEN 7 MEN
TRAPPED ON
AN ISLAND

NOWHERE TO HIDE
NOWHERE TO RUN

TURNING INTO A **HELL** OF
LUST AND **VIOLENCE**

EAGLE FILMS
present

THE RAPE

(CERT X' London)

MEN
OR
BEASTS?
·
WOMEN
OR
WANTONS?

More suffering in *The Rape*.

sors. Fairly graphic it was, too, although even the Greeks held to the convention that while women could strip, men always raped with their trousers on.

The Greeks always used Nazis, Turks or bandits in their rape sequences, as in this most recent film of the new Cypriot cinema, *Hassamboulia of Cyprus*. Buñuel and the Spanish preferred more *outré* surroundings, from the assault by the beggars on *Viridiana* to the violation by the inmates of each other in the Victorian asylum in Alba's *Le Condannate*. Pushing to the frontiers of the bizarre was,

More assault in *Hassamboulia of Cyprus* (above) and *Le Condannate* (below).

naturally, Hammer Films with its teaser posters and an extraordinary sequence later cut from *When Dinosaurs Ruled the Earth,* in which Victoria Vetri was threatened with multiple violation by a giant crab. But it took the Italians to push the bizarre documentary-type violences of *Mondo Cane* to their ultimate conclusion in *Africa Erotica,* where a young American girl is apparently penetrated by most of nature. This film, perhaps more appropriate to the red-light district of Hamburg or the stag party, in fact only received a Restricted rating in America, so that any child could see it if accom-

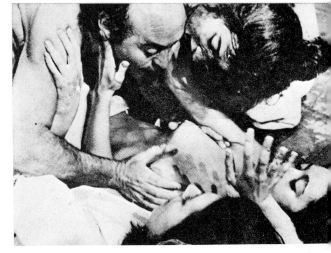

Victoria Vetri under threat in a Hammer vehicle.

Africa Erotica was subtitled 'A Happening in Africa' to appeal to the youth market. Interestingly enough, the chimpanzee was filmed with the girl both half-dressed and not at all – the old double version.

panied by an adult guardian. It was a far cry from Tarzan and Jane, although shot in the genuine Tanzanian wilderness.

By the 1970s, the problem was really where the 'art' film ended and the soft-core or hard-core pornographic film began. One actor, Marlon Brando, had begun the trend towards more shocking rape sequences in *A Streetcar Named Desire*.

It was, incidentally, his depiction of a motorbike gangleader in *The Wild One*, which got the film totally banned in England for many years. Fifteen years later, after something of an eclipse in the 1960s, he again led the way in appearing as a star in a naked sado-masochistic love-scene with Stephanie Beecham in Michael Winner's *The Nightcomers*, which

Brando and Stephanie Beecham in *The Nightcomers* (1971).

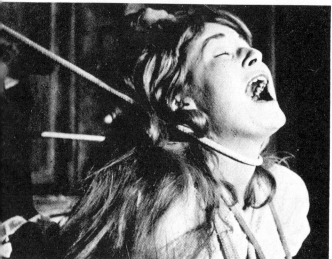

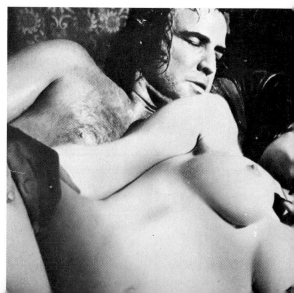

purported to show what took place between the evil Quint and Jessel before the beginning of Henry James's 'The Turn of the Screw'. In the Brando version, it was both violent and sexual. The film proved to be, however, no great success except as a hot run for Brando before the notorious *Last Tango in Paris*, where his earthy dialogue and sodomy scenes with Maria Schneider caused a rumpus and a scissoring of the butter sequence in most countries except America, already inured to more explicit sex on screen and on general release in the Damiani skin-flicks.

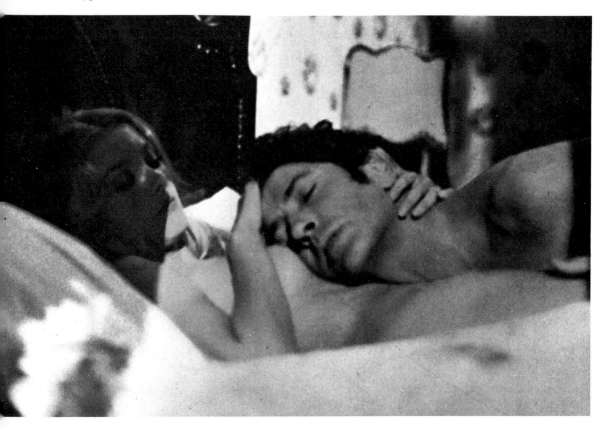

Farley Granger gives up his clean-cut image (above) . . . and Jack Lemmon plays the lady with Marilyn Monroe.

The reason for the change in what could be seen on the general screen was fourfold: the increasing fall in box-office takings because of television, so that the cinema had to offer more than the box; the new frankness and acceptance of nudity by the youth generation of *Woodstock* and after, which made up more than half the market; the need of the ageing stars to play to that youth market; and the fact that most film-makers and distributors will always get away with all they can which is novel, extraordinary and notorious. The collapse of censorship on the matter of screen sex in most capitalist countries outside the Communist and Third Worlds, was due to increasing pressure put on the censors by public criticism, which endlessly reiterated the theme that nakedness and sexual play harmed few by its example, while the violence of war, shown daily on the television newsreels, about Vietnam and Ireland was a worse influence. How could a censor cut out a pair of breasts for an

Lemmon and Juliet Mills in *Avanti*

adult audience when any child could see peasants napalmed to agony on the six o'clock news?

The censors did not allow all. In Europe, they continued to distinguish between the exploitation picture and the serious picture. That is why the presence of the stars was so important. They were held to be incapable, on the whole, of demeaning their reputation. If it was a long walk for the athletic Farley Granger from Hitchcock's *Strangers in the Train* to his latest Italian picture with Rosalba Neri and Barbara Bouchet, *Hot Bed of Sex*, he was only following a well-blazed trail for the ageing star. Billy Wilder, who had made transvestitism fun in his comic masterpiece of the fifties, *Some Like It Hot*, and had made Marilyn Monroe the sex symbol of the world with a bathing suit on, followed the fashion of the seventies in his flop with Jack Lemmon, *Avanti*, in which he asked that ex-symbol of childish purity, Juliet Mills, to put on weight for the part and then to strip and show it in

an unfunny tale about a double adultery. It was sad to see the great Henry Fonda and Glenn Ford reduced to embarrassed naughtiness in *The Rounders*, or Belmondo in the same situation with Laura Antonelli in *Doctor Popaul*. Ursula Andress has escalated her undress since she first achieved stardom with Sean Connery in the Bond pictures; her latest love-scenes are also paralleled by the middle-aged Connery's scenes of rape and dream-sex in *Zardoz*. And so the catalogue continues

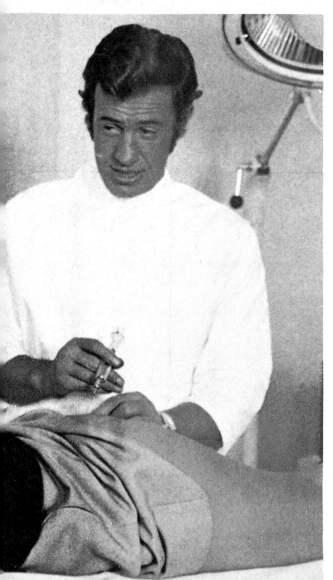

The girl from *Dr. No* and ex-007 Sean Connery go further than the Bond fantasies, especially he in *Zardoz* (1973) (below)

Belmondo looks embarrassed in *Doctor Popoul*.

Mick Jagger, Anita Pallenberg and Michèle Breton increase the possibilities of the traditional bath scene in *Performance* (1970).

Joe Dalessandro in Warhol's *Trash* (1970).

Despite heavy cutting of most of the offensive material and the fact that the film was made by Morrisey (not by Warhol), the English distributors could not resist a teaser poster for *Flesh for Frankenstein* (1975).

with ageing stars and directors revealing more and more in an attempt to hang on to a fickle public, always seeking a further sensation.

For the public remains the final censor. Those who defy age, such as Marlene Dietrich, keep an audience of the old (and the camp young) who relish her longevity of beauty and who dream of achieving half as much. But more appropriate for the young mass audience are the films of their new perverse stars, such as Mick Jagger and Joe Dallesandro. Jagger's bi-sexual role in *Performance* was largely censored by indifferent distribution; its success could probably come with a re-issue after *The Rocky Horror Show,* since its shocks have diminished as the seventies lengthen. Dallesandro, on the other hand, in his Warhol and Morrisey films has risen from the casual full frontal hustler roles of *Flesh* and *Trash* (passed almost without cuts in England) to the international camp classics such as *Flesh for Frankenstein* (savaged to pieces by the new English censor for its three-dimensional confusion of vagina with viscera). Dallesandro's curious resemblance to Valentino, both in physique and in wooden acting, may yet make him a cult among the young – and the censor's nightmare.

The trouble with the Warhol films was that they began to cross the strange borderline between the acceptable spoof and the sexploitation take-off, like *Kiss Me Quick.* A curious and notorious send-up made the national circuits in 1975, *Flesh Gordon. (See Colour Section.)* Its plot had the world ravaged by a sex ray which induced uncontrollable orgies, so that Flesh had to embark with Dale Ardor on Dr. Jerkoff's phallic rocket to combat its source on the planet Porno. But the other send-ups of major movies, such as the absurd *The Notorious Cleopatra,* or the mock-Westerns like *Lash of Lust* or *The Marauders* were really more made for the blue-movie circuit than for mass release. The kicks in them were bondage and sado-masochism at the silly level that distinguishes most pornography.

There had always been three markets for the sex film – the 'art' and general market, the limited sexploitation play-houses that flourished in such neighbourhoods as 42nd Street in New York, and finally the hard-core stag film. While the

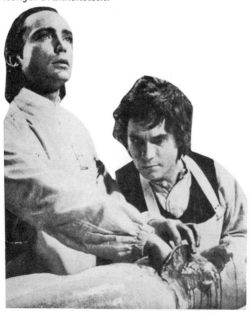

Taken from the visceral rape scenes cut from *Flesh for Frankenstein.*

Joe Dalessandro shows his Valentino aspect to Monique Van Vooren.

While the real *Flash Gordon* is threatened by phallic prongs, *Flesh Gordon* uses the joy-stick of Dr. Jerkoff's rocket.

While the girls tie up the man in *The Notorious Cleopatra,* the threat of a gun makes them drop their Victorian dresses in *Lash of Lush*

... while the cowboy grovels before the bound Queen of the skin-flicks, Uschi Digart, in *The Marauders*.

first market on its posters would not get much beyond *Emanuelle*, the second one moved from the coyness of the forties to more explicit advertising and front-of-house titles such as the sixties' successes, *The House on Bare Mountain, Pardon My Brush, Frantic Fanny, The Touchables, Nautical Nudes, Knockers Up, Scanty Panties, Wild for Kicks, Bachelor Tom Peeping,* and *Satan in High Heels,* which brought in fetishism to bolster a flagging market.

The breakthrough of the pornograph movie into mass release in the United States was the phenomenon of the years after 1973. In nearly every state outside the Deep South, the three Damiani pictures, *Deep Throat* and *Deep Throat Part II* with Linda Lovelace, and *The Devil in Miss Jones* with Georgina Spelvin, grossed millions and openly showed fellatio and sodomy in lingering close-up. The other of the pornographic movies which was widely shown was the Mitchell Brothers' *Behind the Green Door,* where the golden girl Marilyn Chambers had many men simultaneously on trapezes, thus fulfilling an old, male fantasy. This film was banned outright in Europe outside

SF DISTRIBUTORS present

a JUST JAECKIN film

ALAIN CUNY
SYLVIA KRISTEL
MARIKA GREEN

Emmanuelle X

French Dialogue - English Subtitles

DANIEL SARKY · JEANNE COLLETIN · CHRISTINE BOISSON · SAMANTHA music PIERRE BACHELET

Early teaser posters for skin-flicks.

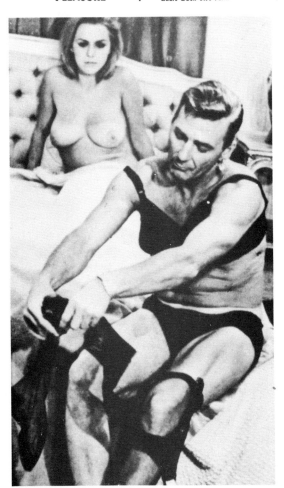

A drag queen from *Satan in High Heels* (1960).

Scandinavia, where such things were thought quaint. In most European countries, the line between the permissible release and the stag film was still chalked in blue, while in the United States, the Saturday Review critic could praise the film as 'sex as ritual, sex as fantasy, sex as it could be only in the movies . . . '. Dependent on censorship, of course.

Perhaps the most mocking view of censorship in the field of sex was taken by the sex films themselves. Axel's *Danish Blue* kidded censorship by showing how to make pornographic movies through the ages – and how to censor them. The American skin-flick *Wild Out-takes* starred veteran film-stripper Bambi Allen as Constance Virtue with the scissors, chipping out the censored sections from other blue movies (which naturally made up this film). Yet, as he so often had, Lenny Bruce had the last word about the problem:

'I never did see one stag film where anybody got killed in the end. Or even slapped in the mouth. Or where it had any Communist propaganda.'

86

From *Deep Throat Part I.*

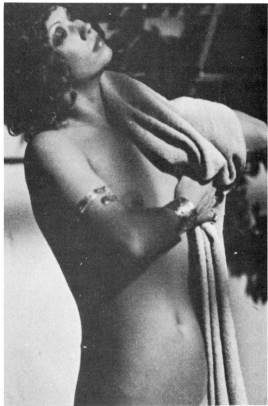

Linda Lovelace has a blade to put in her famous mouth in Deep Throat, Part II, while Georgina Spelvin plays Bathsheba (above), and Marilyn Chambers performs (below).

"BEHIND the GREEN DOOR"

"...it is sex as ritual, sex as fantasy, sex as it could be only in the movies..."
ARTHUR KNIGHT
SATURDAY REVIEW

"Miss Chambers is a 20-year old lovely fresh-faced 'innocent'... who does everything quite realistically."
JIM HARWOOD
VARIETY

"In terms of lighting, photography, technical experimentation and erotic content, it stands pretty much alone."
JOHN WASSERMAN
S.F. CHRONICLE

"Behind the Green Door" is an erotic classic. It is almost more a woman's film than a man's, and several women I know who have seen it say "At last!"
WILLIAM ROTSLER
ADAM MAGAZINE

The old-fashioned censors enjoy themselves in *Danish Blue*.

A wild out-take from *Wild-Out-takes*.

cut on violence

The Crucifixion was the worst blasphemy. It was the violent death of the Son of God. The image of the cross inspired and haunted the minds of the Middle Ages. Both its power and its blasphemy were also bound to haunt the images of the new makers of pictures.

In its earliest use, the Cross stood for both redemption for Mary Pickford as *The Little American* caught by the First World War, also for blasphemy in this early film of a flagellant cult in New Mexico, called *The Penitente*. Sometimes it was used for torture, as in the St. Andrew's Cross of the 1923 version of the *Hunchback of Notre Dame*. Sometimes it was used for religious and sexual symbolism (as well as bondage) by American producers of the scale of de Mille, while Eisenstein used it for anti-religious propoganda in the cause of Bolshevism. In Visconti's *Rocco and his Brothers,* Annie Giradot offered herself as an Italian sacrificial victim for the 1960s, while a Brazilian painter had a vision of the Inferno even more extreme than earlier film versions of Dante's. At each stage, the symbol of the Cross became more commonplace and therefore had to be presented more outrageously, as it lost its power to awe and shock by the repetition of the image. Thus by 1975, the Cross had to be restored

The early use of the Cross as blasphemy . . . and torture.

Annie Giradot in *Rocco and his Brothers* (1960).

Loretta Young gives the sword as Cross a
religious and sexual significance in de Mille's
The Crusades (1935).

The Inferno scene from José Mojica Marins' *Esta Nocte Encarnerei Seu Cadaver* (1966).

A scene from Peter Fleischmann's *Dorethea* about the way in which a seventeen-year-old girl looks at the world.

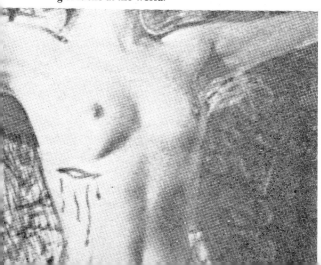

from its black mark on a Censor's Certificate – the X film – to its original meaning of bloody violence and blasphemy in order to affect its viewers, as in the recent German political film *Dorethea* (successful in Paris, banned in London) or in Marcel Hanoun's use of an old religious fantasy, that of a woman imagining her body as Christ's.

Although the symbol of the crucifixion was used seriously in all these cases, it has remained a staple image in Catholic countries where blasphemy excites sexually. Jean Rollin used its image when he largely invented the French sex-vampire film; and in Italy, where the sight of the naked nun is still the ultimate in outrage, the shot of the crucified or violated or humiliated nun is still the ultimate crowd-pleaser at the box-office because of its appeal to erotic fantasies. Very often, this situation is played lightly, as in the charming Bardot film with Annie Giradot, *The Novices,* where indeed the novice saves the street-walker for the church – and prays on the beach in a bikini in between.

Using the nun's fantasy about taking the place of Christ, Hanoun literally substitutes the wounded body in *La Verité sur L'Imaginaire d'un Inconnu.*

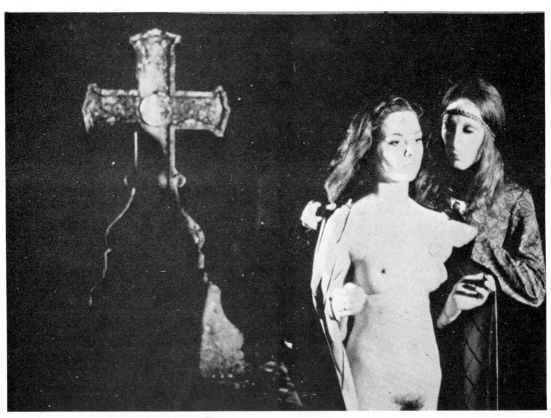

A scene from a Jean Rollin sex-vampire film.

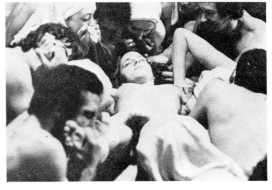

These shots from a recent Florinda Bolkan
vehicle, *Flavia and the Moslems,* indulge
Italian sexual fantasies as does this shot of
humiliation from a recent Anne Heywood vehicle,
Dominici's *The Nuns of Sant'Arcangelo.*

Bardot tries to save Giradot on the beach in *The Novices*.

A medieval mouth of hell.

Yet it was an obsessive English director, Ken Russell, who made the most violent and blasphemous and censorable film in existence, *The Devils* (1971). It deliberately used the outrage of the crucifixion and the sexual dreams of nuns to assault complacency and morality. Russell has recently been called the Hieronymous Bosch of the musical in *Tommy*. He certainly had already been the Bosch of the church. No medieval painting of Hell exceeded Russell's images of sexual degradation – and the crucifixion of the suffering Oliver Reed, playing Urbain Grandier, both in the fantasies of his mistress and the reali-

In this scene of the nuns' exorcism in *The Devils* (1971), scissored nearly everywhere, Ken Russell could not decide whether he was Bosch or Busby Berkeley.

Oliver Reed as the imaginary Christ and as the burned heretic in *The Devils*.

ties of the stake. But it was the antics of the naked nuns, possessed with devils of obscenity and blasphemy, which brought out the censors all over the world in an orgy of hacking the sequences of the madnesses. *(See Colour Section)*.

Russell went as far as he could go in outrage in *The Devils*. At least, it is difficult to imagine a further blasphemous recess in the obsessional mind. The censors of the world (outside that Catholic

The nuns assault the Examiners and the taste of the audience in *The Devils*.

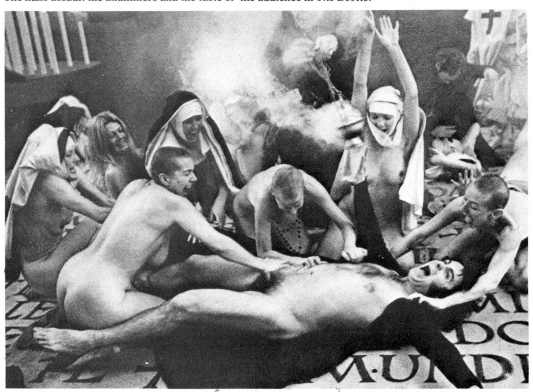

Bruce's excuse for sex on film: 'I would rather my child see a stag film than *The Ten Commandments* or *King of Kings* – because I don't want my kids to kill Christ when he comes back. That's what they see in those films – that violence.' In *The Devils*, the audience not only saw an escalation of de Mille's talent for orgiastic violence, but also the crucifixion, torture and burning of Oliver Reed, and the whipping and torture of hordes of nuns. If there was ever a case for the total ban of a film for religious and social reasons, *The Devils* was that film – and it passed even the censors at Venice despite the Vatican.

The Devils went on mass release nearly everywhere in the capitalist world. Its sado-masochism against women was widely imitated, even if it could not be escalated. The barriers of decency were down now and standards dropped with them. The official censors were besieged with sado-masochism, which they passed if the film was meant to have 'quality' or a moral message like *Soldier Blue*, which began and ended in a sickening massacre

bastion Spain) were so bully-ragged by popular demands for permissiveness that nine-tenths of the film survived the choppers, excused by Aldous Huxley's intent in his original novel *The Devils of Loudon* and by Russell's equivocal seriousness.

Russell had, after all, equated sex with sado-masochistic violence, as in a horrific scene where doctors blister a woman to drive out devils or the plague. Thus he had put himself beyond even Lenny

Stained with the blood of the innocent

soldier blue

JOSEPH E. LEVINE presents an AVCO EMBASSY FILM · A RALPH NELSON PICTURE
starring CANDICE BERGEN · PETER STRAUSS · DONALD PLEASENCE · JOHN ANDERSON · DANA ELCAR
From the novel Arrow in the Sun by THEODORE V. OLSEN · Executive Producer JOSEPH E. LEVINE · Music by ROY BUDD · Title Song by BUFFY SAINTE-MARIE · Screenplay by JOHN GAY
Produced by HAROLD LOEB and GABRIEL KATZKA · Directed by RALPH NELSON · Prints by MOVIELAB · TECHNICOLOR® PANAVISION®   AN AVCO EMBASSY RELEASE

Catherine Deneuve . . . and Charlotte Rampling
suffer from Nazi persecution.

The girls do not suffer too much in the Freudian cinema such as the girl who enjoys daggers in America's *Odd Tastes*, Marijke Boonstra strapped to the shower in the Dutch *Obsessions*, Catherine Spaak chained to a chest in the Italian *The Libertine*, and Krista Nell also chained in the French *Eros Thanatos*.

Artists and models, modern Prague and Paris style.

Attack á la Bunuel and á la Pallardy. (below right)

Yet these films could have, or pretend to have, a reason for their sado-masochism. Most of such films merely showed the poor taste of public and their makers, who catered for the market and tried to slip the films past the official censors wherever they could. Those who pandered to their special audience did not hide their purposes now, calling the films such names as *Odd Tastes* and *Obsessions* and *Eros Thanatos* and *The Libertine*. It was overt Freudian cinema with a vengeance, even when it was more surrealism than exploitation, such as in the two charming films on sculptors, the Czech *The Most Beautiful Age* and the French *De Mes Amours Decomposées*, which went back to the old device of artist and model, and did not *really* use the calipers or the chisel on their subjects.

Not so in the more sado-erotic section of the market, where the official censors still watched and cut. While Bunuel's *Belle de Jour*, for instance, did see the rich *bourgeois* housewife whipped and spattered with mud and working in a brothel

— its poster was the old teaser, now passable on mass release. The Nazis were a good excuse for showing sado-masochism with historical justification and a moral message. Catherine Deneuve played their victim in Vadim's *Vice and Virtue*, while Charlotte Rampling played their unwilling and willing victim in *The Night Porter*, performing a cabaret dance seminaked in uniform that outdid even Marlene Dietrich in *The Blue Angel*.

Catherine Deneuve dreams her fantasies in *Belle de Jour* (1967) . . .

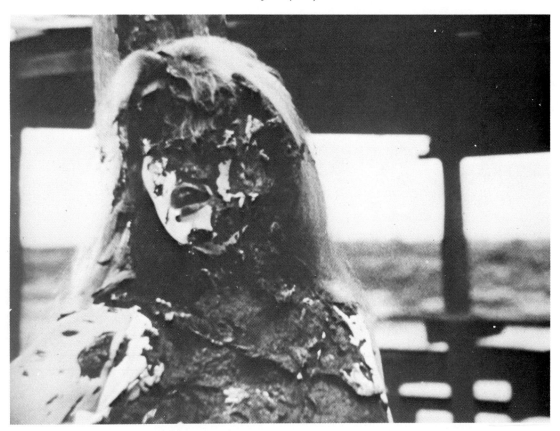

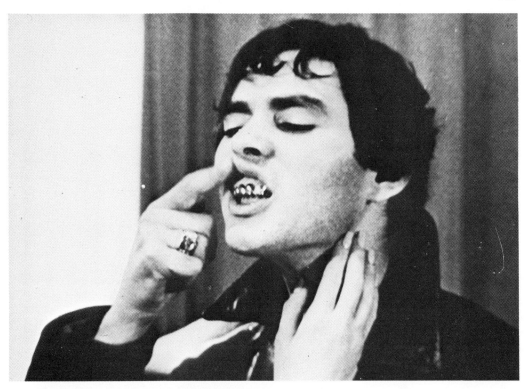

. . . and acts them out in the brothel with Pierre Clementi.

to live out her fantasies, an imitator such as Rossatti's *Wife by Night* provided half the eroticism and twice the sadism by showing too much in a world which Buñuel had pioneered in his early Surrealist days. It was the same with Buñuel's *Discreet Charm of the Bourgeoisie*, which won worldwide attention by its velvet-knife assault on middle-class principles, while its lesser imitators such as Pallardy's *Erotic Dossier of a Notary* relied far more on sadism than surrealism to make their points. Even Mai Zetterling made a sad mess of a promising career as a film director in her *Night Games*, heavily censored after its opening at the Venice Festival.

To act out sexual obsessions on the screen was not enough. They had to be done well and to be done for a point, in context and in character. Yet Lenny Bruce was right – it was the violence that shocked, not the perversion. The Italian cinema, with its long tradition of sacrificial victims of Roman circuses, most frequently employed sexual sadism for the home

Eva Czemerys does the same in *Wife by Night*.

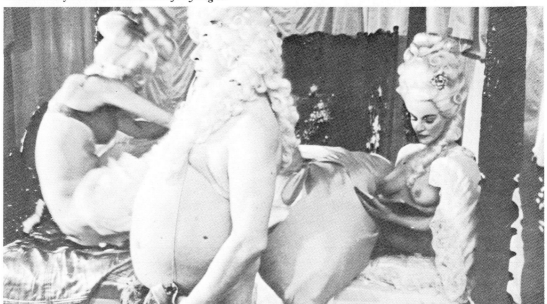

A sexual fantasy acted out in *Night Games*.

product – it was cut for the overseas market. After watching the assault scenes in Ralli's *Desperate Moments* or in Ercoli's *Death Walks in High-Heeled Shoes*, one might ask what the Italian male was afraid of, that he could only approach women with a knife. *(See Colour Section.)*

Torture had, indeed, had a long public tradition as a spectacle, as was shown by the massive crowds at the medieval pillory and execution, and the later witch-burnings. The Museums with their instruments from the Middle Ages provided much of the inspiration for the art directors, who wished to satisfy the blood-lust of the mass audience. Trials for witchcraft were the most satisfactory way of showing the torture of women to a willing market. From classics like *The Hunchback of Notre Dame* to endless versions of naked virgins suffering from Satanists, who then suffered from the hands of the Inquisition, the world of film witchcraft gave an outlet for the suppressed violence of millions of men – where the censors allowed it to be shown.

In a notorious and scissored sequence from a Barbara Steele film, *The Curse of Crimson Altar* (1968), the Devil-worshippers flog the victim.

Gina Lollobrigida suffers the torture of the boot in Delannoy's *The Hunchback of Notre Dame*, Olivera Vuco is examined for refusing the witchfinder in *Austria, 1700,* while Gaby Fuchs is put on the rack for witchcraft and blasphemy in Armstrong's *Mark of the Devil*.

As their record in the Second World War seemed to demonstrate, Japanese men had a particular need for breaking out of their excessive obedience by outbursts of violence. The escape in Japan from the extraordinary discipline of the factory appears to be steam baths in the evening and the catharsis of films of incredible sex-and-violence that no censor

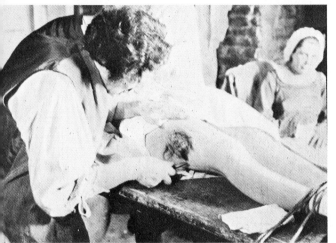

The tell-tale patch of devil's fur is cut off the thigh of one of the witch maidens in Haggard's *Satan's Skin* (1972).

could pass outside Japan. Occasionally, one of these films reaches Paris, such as Wakamatsu Koji's *The Embryo* or Kiyumori Suzuki's *Gate of Flesh*, shown in Belgium. They are distinguished by an overt pleasure in sadism that few censors would permit in Europe. As Koji says, 'For me, violence, the body and sex are an integral part of life' – and of profits in the cinema. There are practically no straight sex films in Japan; all contain aggression, blood and perversion.

What is shown on the screen and where it is shown depends on the nature of each country. If Japan reaches the outer limits of permissiveness (closely followed by Scandinavia and now by the United States), the Communist World and South Africa and Spain and Eire remain on guard for whatever is thought filthy or subversive in the movies. At the last resort, indeed, the films made in each country depend more on the makers than on the official censors, who may only see the final product. In Greece, for example, under the puritan régime of the Colonels, a sex-film industry flourished, entirely for

Scenes from Suzuki's *Gate of Flesh* (1968).

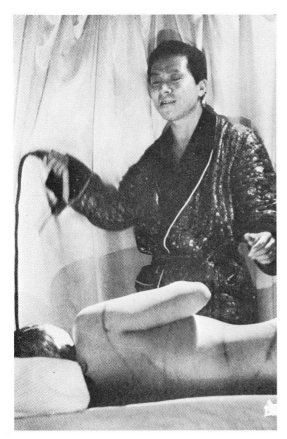

Scenes from Koji's *The Embryo* (1966).

This scene was cut from *Double Indemnity* . . . And from *Can-Can* on general release.

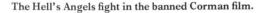

The Hell's Angels fight in the banned Corman film.   **The gentlemen try a kiss in the shelved Kotcheff movie.**

export. It was the financiers of these films who had them made and had them shown elsewhere. Without the money, no films. And without the distribution, no money back for more films.

So the real censors of the cinema remain the financiers and the distributors, often the same people. Theirs is the initial and final sabotage of what we see. In *Double Indemnity*, for instance, the last scene of Edward G. Robinson watching Fred MacMurray die in the gas chamber was cut by the distributors on general release, as was the famous Apache dance from *Can-Can* with Shirley Maclaine – even Krushchev on his only visit to Hollywood had thought the film indecent.

Many films were never shown at all in various countries, either because they were thought to be socially undesirable or financially unprofitable. In the days when motor-bike gangs terrorised the imagination even more than the sea-coast resorts of England, Brando's *The Wild One* and Corman's *The Wild Angels* were completely banned from Britain. Yet for every single film banned by the official censor, the distributors inexplicably banned or shelved two more. The reasons are obscure, from apparent racial squeamishness in the case of Kotcheff's *Two Gentlemen Sharing* to a studio shake-up and apparent political squeamishness in the case of Sinclair's updated *The*

A waxwork of Winston Churchill gets his face burned in revenge for the Dresden raid (seen in *Slaughterhouse Five*) and the Guards confront the skinheads in *The Breaking of Bumbo* (1970).

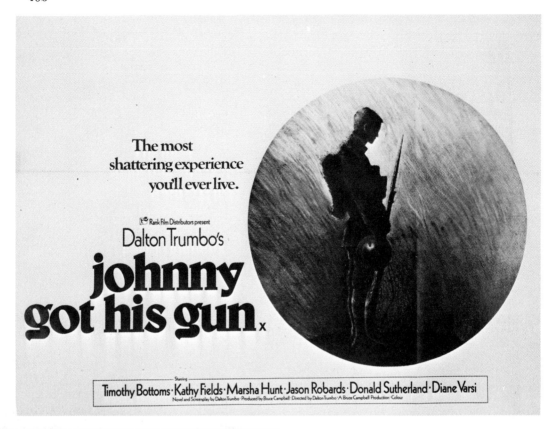

The most
shattering experience
you'll ever live.

Rank Film Distributors present

Dalton Trumbo's

johnny got his gun. x

Starring
Timothy Bottoms · Kathy Fields · Marsha Hunt · Jason Robards · Donald Sutherland · Diane Varsi
Novel and Screenplay by Dalton Trumbo · Produced by Bruce Campbell · Directed by Dalton Trumbo · A Bruce Campbell Production · Colour

The priest puts the devil in hell in Pasolini's
***The Decameron* (1970).**

Breaking of Bumbo. The distributors' reasons for shelving a film that has cost a small fortune are always financial – distribution costs may make the release of a film worthless, or else a total tax-loss write-off may suit the cash-flow of the distribution company. Yet this argument is often a cloak for censorship on moral or political grounds – or because of sheer ego.

Yet often the distributors are proved right. Where there is an outcry from a literate minority to show such a violent anti-war movie as Trumbo's version of *Johnny Got His Gun*, in which the soldier hero is left totally blind, deaf, dumb and limbless to recollect his life, the public will simply not go and support the film. While money rules what is made and what is shown, the money paid by the cinema audience is the final arbiter. And the censors with their choppers sit as uneasy judges between the pressures of the film financiers and protests of the moralists, trying like politicians to keep out of trouble and trim only enough to keep the victim alive at the box-office and the censor in his salaried job.

Recently in London there has been a move – narrowly defeated – to abolish the need for censorship in the films shown in the London area. The arguments on both sides were monotonously the same, with the purveyors of soft pornography backing the moralists in wishing to keep

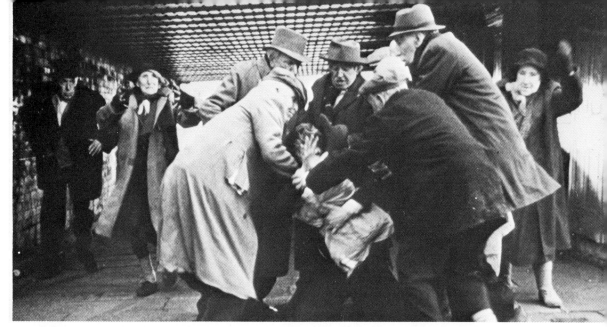

In Kubrick's shattering *The Clockwork Orange,* the droogs attack the tramps, the tramps have their revenge on the brainwashed Malcolm McDowell, and finally he has an orgiastic vision of sex and shocking society, when restored to his anarchic nature.

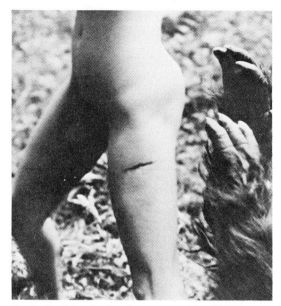

The body of the shepherdess menaced by the beast in *Immoral Tales* (1974). In this, the raped girl wears out her bestial attacker through her lust. The phallic arrow is fired by Ninetto Davoli at Luigeana Rocchi in *The Arabian Nights*. (below)

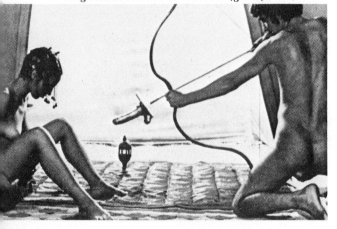

their product safe (and scissored) from the competition of the purveyors of hard pornography backing the liberals in letting the people choose what they wanted to patronise. Both sides over-used the word 'freedom', either the freedom from being swamped in a flood of skin and violence, or the freedom to be swamped if one wished. Like the battles of the priest and the devil, this was to be an unresolved contest (ignoring the *Decameron* tale where the priest manages to convince the peasant's wife that the devil can be put away in hell for ever, by a very old method).

The real crux of the question of censorship lies in whether the graphic portrayal of violence and sexual perversion incites its audience to perform the same acts in real life. For every psychiatrist or social worker who says that films corrupt and provoke on one side, another psychiatrist or social worker will say that films release and assuage on the other side. It is rare that there are actual happenings, as after the mass release of *A Clockwork Orange*, where gangs of boys do set old tramps alight dressed in the bowler hats of the droogs. Yet for every single case of such

Count Zaroff assembles his hunters to hunt the two lovers in *The Most Dangerous Game* (1931).

anti-social horror, there were millions who were moved by the film in its unsparing presentation of the oldest dilemma in the world – should men be left to be free and sometimes evil, or should they be programmed to be good and slavish?

So the censorship of films has reverted by 1975 to its position before the First World War. 'This isn't a business,' as the distributor said, 'it's a dissipation.' However highly organised modern distributors were, the collapse of the old Hollywood studio system linked to distribution and the supremacy of television left the field open for the outrageous and the novel. Outside Japan, could a film on gluttony go further than *Blow Out*, a film on violence exceed *Weekend* or *Point Blank*, a film on lust and bestiality show more than *The Arabian Nights* or Borowczyk's *Immoral Tales*, or a film blaspheme more verbally than *Last Tango in Paris* or visually than *Dorethea*? Presumably there are new excesses to plumb, new human obsessions to depict, but the search for the weird inglenooks of human nature seems to be reaching its limits.

Arrabal has taken over from Buñuel as the leading spear-carrier of surrealism, and the urge to shock a time beyond shock. He appears as an actor in *Piège*, a recent film by Jacques Baratier, inspired by that grand-daddy of the sadistic cinema, the manhunt of the lovers by Count Zaroff in *The Most Dangerous Game*. In the film, a thief played by Bulle Ogier is put in a trap by another thief, Bernadette Lafont, who plays the evil Zaroff role of the torturer in black to Ogier's victim in white. Arrabal himself plays the seller of man-traps and animal-traps, and he provides the philosophy of sadism and masochism in the cinema, refusing the designations and stating that all depictions of outrage and violence are only the fight of good against evil in the human personality, which is born aggressive and erotic and suffering. As for those who choose to censor such material by using the scissors on it, by not distributing it, or by not paying their money to see it, the maker Jacques Baratier has the final words on all censorship:

'At the last count, this film is a trap – its only victims are those who find it filthy. All pornography is imaginary. It is the folklore of masochism. Vicious is he who is offended by it. Happy is he who delights in it.'

Arrabal plays with a trap in Baratier's *Piège*, while Bulle Ogier is the victim.